Nia Ellis

GW01418926

The Project Research Pack

David Wray

Stanley Thornes (Publishers) Ltd

© David Wray 1991

Cartoons by Andrew Keylock.

Illustrations by Tim Hayward.

The copyright holders authorise ONLY users of *The Project Research Pack* to make photocopies or stencil duplicates of these masters for their own, or their classes', immediate use within the teaching context.

No other rights are granted without permission in writing from the publisher or under licence from the Copyright Licensing Agency Limited. Further details of such licences (for reprographic reproduction) may be obtained from the Copyright Licensing Agency Limited, 33–4 Alfred Place, London WC1E 7DP.

Copy by any other means or for any other purpose is strictly prohibited without the prior consent of the copyright holders.

Applications for such permission should be addressed to the publishers: Stanley Thornes (Publishers) Ltd, Old Station Drive, Leckhampton, CHELTENHAM GL53 0DN, England.

First published in 1991 by Stanley Thornes (Publishers) Ltd, Old Station Drive, Leckhampton, CHELTENHAM GL53 0DN, UK.

British Library Cataloguing in Publication Data

Wray, David, 1950–
    The project research pack.
    1. Primary schools. Projects
    I. Title
    372.136

    ISBN 0–7487–0434–5

Typeset by Tech-Set, Gateshead, Tyne & Wear.
Printed in Great Britain at The Bath Press, Avon.

Contents

Teaching notes

INTRODUCTION

The Project Research Pack consists of a set of photocopiable activity sheets to be used as a resource with primary children working on particular projects. The sheets have two distinctive features:

1   They are resources for project work. A teacher working on a particular project can select appropriate sheets from the pack to support and extend the work.

2   They are focused specifically on the development of information skills, thus enabling a systematic programme of development to be worked out.

RATIONALE

Research has indicated that the area of information skills is much neglected, especially in primary schools. Consequently, many schools expect their children to use information in quite sophisticated ways, particularly in project work, without ensuring that the requisite skills are taught. Criticisms of project work as a teaching activity, which suggest it consists largely of haphazard, 'uninvolved copying', stem from this situation.

The demands of the National Curriculum include the teaching of information skills, which forms part of the *Attainment Target for Reading* (DES, 1989), although the accompanying programmes of study are less than helpful in suggesting ways of teaching these skills. Their requirements are limited to the statement that:

> pupils should learn how to locate information in books and, where available, databases, sometimes drawing on more than one source, and how to pursue an independent line of enquiry.

Some schools have already recognised the need to teach information skills, but have attempted to do so through special lessons or exercises. These attempts have been supported by published materials with such titles as *Study Skills* and *Reading for Learning*. The problem with materials such as these is their decontextualised nature. Children may not see the reason for doing the activities, and there may be very limited transfer of learning. It has been suggested (Wray, 1985) that more effective learning would occur if this teaching were embedded in contexts which were meaningful and interesting to children in their own right. Project work would therefore seem to be the ideal context in which such skills should be taught for several reasons:

— Children are usually highly motivated to do it and they are often prepared to take a great deal of trouble to do well at something in which they are interested.

— The project has a rationale of its own and any skills which are practised as part of it are there because they are needed to complete the project. Skills teaching is therefore applied rather than decontextualised.

— Skills can be taught and practised using material which is thoroughly appropriate to them, rather than specially devised and, because of that, often a little 'unreal'.

While all this is true, it may still leave teachers with little support beyond their own imagination for ensuring that the requisite skills are taught during project work. These sheets therefore provide a set of activities which teachers can use during project work as interesting avenues for exploration, but which are also focused specifically on particular information skills.

THE DESIGN OF THE MATERIALS

The materials cover 12 popular project titles and for each of these there are nine activity sheets covering the range of information skills. Thus within any of the project packs there is sufficient material to enable the full range of information skills to be covered.

A   Range of projects
The 12 project titles are:

    Homes and Houses
    The Vikings
    Transport
    Dinosaurs
    Food
    The Romans
    Animals
    Our town
    Holidays
    Space
    The Weather
    Communications

B   Range of skills
The skills to be covered are those classified as the six stages in the information process (Wray, 1985). These stages are given below and matched with statements of attainment from the National Curriculum English.

1	Defining subject and purpose of enquiry	Devise a clear set of questions that will enable them to select and use appropriate information sources. (Reading: level 3)

2	Locating information	Locate books or magazines in the class or school library by using the classification system or catalogue. (Reading: level 4)
3	Selecting information	Select reference books and other information materials, and use organisational devices to find answers to their own questions. (Reading: level 5)
4	Organising information	Organise non-chronological writing in orderly ways. (Writing: level 4)
5	Evaluating information	Recognise, in discussion, whether subject matter in non-literary and media texts is presented as fact or as opinion. (Reading: level 5)
6	Communicating information	Produce pieces of writing in which there is a rudimentary attempt to present simple subject matter in a structured way. (Writing: level 4)

There are sheets covering the first five of these stages in each of the 12 project sections. For the sixth stage, 'Communicating information', there are six content-free sheets which can be used in any project as appropriate. These are placed in the 'Presentation activities' section at the end of the book.

C   Levels of difficulty

To enable most teachers of junior children to use the materials, the activity sheets cover two broad levels of difficulty. Roughly half the sheets are suitable for children of lower junior age and half for those of upper junior age. This is indicated to the teacher in the teaching notes for each project, but not on the sheets themselves to allow for maximum flexibility of use. It should be emphasised that this is a tentative grading only and teachers are urged to use the sheets in a manner determined by the needs of their particular children.

EXPECTED CLASSROOM USE

The sheets are intended as a *resource* for project work, to be used when judged appropriate by teachers. There is no intention to provide material for the comprehensive coverage of any project.

Each group of sheets is accompanied by teaching notes which give suggestions for their use.

Some of the sheets will work well as individual activities, although most will benefit from being done collaboratively by small groups of two to four children. The majority will benefit from some discussion with the children before they tackle the activities.

You might wish to ensure beforehand that there are sufficient suitable reference books easily available to the children. Whether these are pre-selected for them, or have to be found by them in larger collections or libraries, will depend on the maturity of the children and their mastery of particular skills. It is best not to attempt to ensure that every piece of information they will need is actually present in the books they have. Children need the experience that adults get regularly: finding that the information they require is not easily located, and might need further research. If particular items of information are hard to locate, the children might need to go elsewhere to look, for example, at home, or in the town library.

Discuss with them how they will use the reference books. Make sure that the use of both the contents page, and an index is discussed. Model the correct use of these for them, and then get a child to demonstrate for the rest. They will then be ready to begin the activities.

MONITORING THE ACTIVITY

It is worthwhile keeping an eye on the strategies the children adopt to complete the sheets. Try to observe them from time to time, as unobtrusively as possible. Make a note of their use of the sources of information, perhaps using the photocopiable check-list included in the pack (see page 4).

FOLLOWING UP

It is very useful to have a debriefing session after each activity has been completed. Discuss with the children how they tackled the exercise and whether they found any problems. The emphasis here will not be on correct answers but on how they went about finding them. Take the opportunity to reinforce the skills of using sources of information which the children have been practising.

RELATED ACTIVITIES

There are numerous other ways these skills can be practised in the context of a project. Here are a few suggestions:

1   Design quizzes about the topic for the children to complete. Better still, let the children design quizzes for each other. These quizzes could be organised competitively.

2   Get the children to produce fact-sheets about particular topics. Discuss with them beforehand what facts should be on the fact-sheets and compile lists of guideline questions and sample formats.

3 Design (or get the children to design) topic crosswords in which the answers to the clues can be found by consulting reference books.

4 Discuss ways of presenting information to a variety of audiences.

5 Let children experiment with formats for presenting information, and try them out. Encourage revision and redrafting.

Other ideas will be found in Wray (1985) as listed below.

REFERENCES

DES, *English for ages 5 to 16*, HMSO, 1989.
Wray, D., *Teaching Information Skills through Project Work*, Hodder and Stoughton, 1985.

Reading performance checklist

Name _____

Skill for assessment	Points to look for. Can he or she . . .	Performance
Setting goals	. . . specify aims? . . . specify an audience?	
Defining specific purposes	. . . set questions for investigation? . . . organise work?	
Locating information	. . . find information sources? . . . use these sources?	
Using books	. . . assess appropriate books? . . . find information in books?	
Using appropriate reading strategy	. . . skim, scan, and understand what is read?	
Using information	. . . take notes? . . . present information effectively?	
Evaluation of work	. . . evaluate work? . . . suggest improvements?	

Notes about each of these skill areas can be made using a simple code such as

/ Introduced to skill
X Some competence
* Competent

or more detailed notes can be made.

© David Wray 1991, *The Project Research Pack*, Stanley Thornes (Publishers) Ltd

Activities

Homes and houses

USING THE ACTIVITIES

The appropriateness of these activities for particular groups of children will depend upon a number of things, including their previous experience with this kind of work. Teachers are therefore urged to use the activity sheets as they think appropriate. Most of the sheets for this topic will be found more suitable for upper junior children, although Activities 3, 4 and, perhaps, 5 are probably within the capabilities of lower juniors.

These activities can be done as self-contained exercises, but they will all benefit greatly from discussion beforehand, and (especially) afterwards. All the sheets will work best if tackled by two or three children together.

In the case of Activities 3, 4, 5 and 6 discussion will be needed beforehand to point out the use of reference sources to the children, and afterwards to draw their attention to the way they were able to use these sources. For Activities 2, 7 and 8 the use of alternative information sources will also need to be discussed. These sheets could form the starting point for a topic on house building and buying in its own right, involving perhaps a visit to a building site and a look at plans etc.

SKILLS TO BE DEVELOPED

Activity 1
This activity is intended to start children thinking about the subject of the project. It focuses particularly upon the asking of questions; a stage all project work should begin with. This activity could be the preliminary to a much larger activity as children attempt to write their own book about an aspect of their project.

Activity 2
The children are here asked to put themselves into someone else's shoes and to ask appropriate questions. It would be particularly useful for them to involve their parents or other adults in this activity. This would broaden their own perspective. This activity links with later work they might do on estate agents.

Activity 3
This is a straightforward information finding and matching task. It focuses particularly upon the use of an index to locate information.

Activity 4
Another information–location task which will require the use of indexes and/or dictionaries. Children are asked at the end to design their own crosswords, an activity which has a great deal of potential.

Answers
Across: 1 Hedges   3 Kennels   7 Broad
  9 Set   11 Hive   12 Of
Down: 2 Den   4 Eyrie   5 Earth   6 Sea
  8 Drey   10 To

Activity 5
This activity again requires the location of particular information. The children will be looking for dates and this provides a good opportunity to introduce them to the technique of scanning – that is, glancing quickly at a page to find a specific piece of information. The drawing up of a time-line might be difficult for some of them and may require some preliminary work.

Activity 6
This activity requires children to select carefully from a range of information that they find, and then to present this information in a prescribed format. It will almost certainly need prior discussion to orientate the children to what they are looking for.

Activity 7
Children are introduced to the flow-chart. If they have not encountered flow-charts before, the idea will require some discussion. It could be suggested to them that they might like to cut up the sheet so as to be able to physically rearrange the elements of the chart.

Activity 8
An activity which focuses upon the evaluation of information. In order to do it properly the children will need further experience of reading and discussing estate agents' descriptions. They might compile, in groups, a collection of typical phrases used in these leaflets. The experience of trying to write to persuade others is very valuable in alerting the writers to the ways others try to persuade them.

Activity 9
A further evaluation activity. Children are asked to decide whether or not they believe things that they read in their books. This will be found quite difficult by most children of junior age and they will need a great deal of discussion and support to do this activity.

Skills analysis

Topic: Homes	Skill stage				
	1	2	3	4	5
Activity 1	√				
Activity 2	√				
Activity 3		√			
Activity 4		√			
Activity 5		√	√		
Activity 6		√	√	√	
Activity 7				√	
Activity 8					√
Activity 9					√

Be an author

A person who writes books is called an author. I am an author. I am writing a book about the history of houses.

The first thing I have to do is to decide what kinds of things I want to say in my book and what sections it will have. The sections of a book are called chapters.

I decided that my book will have these chapters.

Contents

1   Prehistoric living places

2   The first houses

3   Houses in early Britain

4   Houses in the Middle Ages

5

6

7

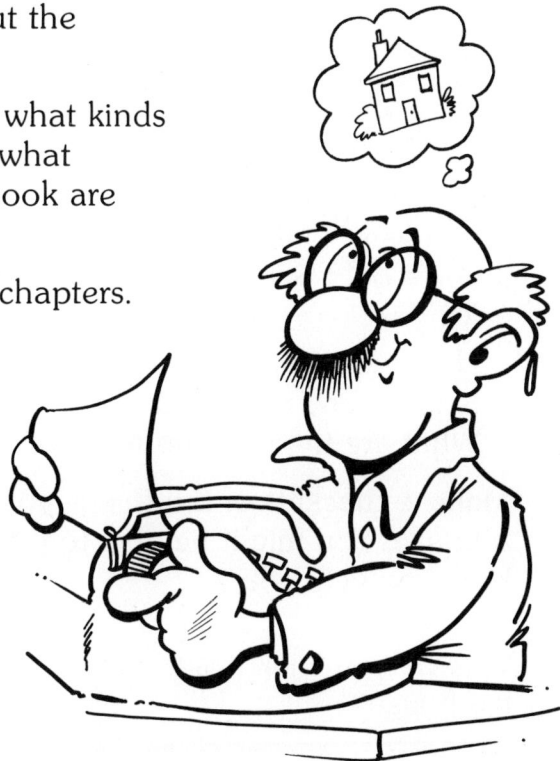

What other chapters do you think I should have in my book? I can think of at least three other chapters to include. What do you think they should be?

Suppose you were an author writing a book on either:
Animal homes
Homes of the future
Special homes.

What chapters would you include in your book?

© David Wray 1991, *The Project Research Pack*, Stanley Thornes (Publishers) Ltd

Buying a house

Activity 2

If you were going to buy a house what would you look for?

With your friends, talk about the things you would really like in a house you were buying.

If you were looking around a house to see if you liked it enough to buy it you would ask the people who lived there lots of questions. You might ask:

How old is the house?
Is there any rot or woodworm in the house?
What are the neighbours like?

Make a checklist of the things you would want to ask if *you* were buying a house. You might be able to get an adult who has actually bought a house to help you.

Why do you think it is important to ask questions like this before you buy the house?

Checklist
1
2
3
4
5
6
7
8

© David Wray 1991, *The Project Research Pack*, Stanley Thornes (Publishers) Ltd

Homes around the world

Can you match up these lists by drawing lines from each type of house to the country in which you would be most likely to find it? The first one has been done for you. Can you identify the types of houses in the drawings?

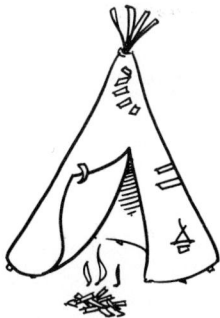

Igloo	North America
Teepee	Spain
Mansion	Scotland
Pagoda	Greenland
Kraal	Britain
Hacienda	China
Croft	Africa

Can you add to the list by thinking of some other types of houses and the countries they belong to?

© David Wray 1991, *The Project Research Pack*, Stanley Thornes (Publishers) Ltd

Animal homes

Can you complete the crossword below by answering the questions? All the answers have something to do with the homes of certain animals. You will find reference books useful for this. Remember to use the index.

CLUES

Across

1 Birds often build nests in these.
3 Dogs live in these.
7 The name for a lake in Norfolk which is home to many birds.
9 A badger lives in one of these.
11 You will find one of these in an apiary.
12 A stable is the home ＿＿＿ a horse.

Down

2 A bear makes its home in one of these.
4 An eagle lives in one of these high up in mountains.
5 The name for the home of a fox.
6 This is home to many animals, especially fish.
8 A squirrel builds one of these in a tree.
10 When cows are not in fields they often go ＿＿＿ a byre.

Perhaps you can design your own crossword puzzle using words which have something to do with homes and houses. See if your friends can solve it.

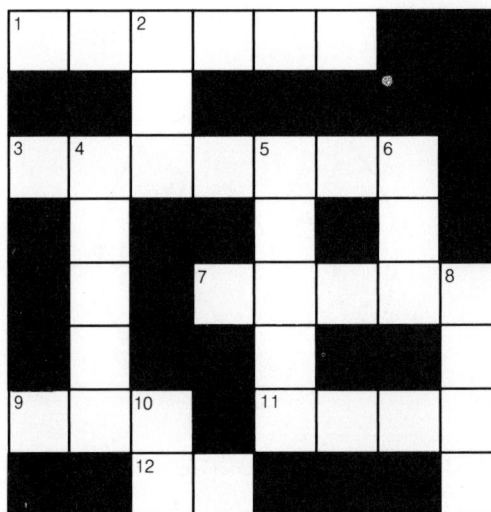

© David Wray 1991, *The Project Research Pack*, Stanley Thornes (Publishers) Ltd

The history of houses

Activity 5

Here are some important events in the history of houses in Britain. Unfortunately they are in the wrong order. Can you rearrange them so that the event which happened first is placed first, and so on? Remember to use the index pages of your reference books to help you.

The Romans begin building villas in Britain.

Houses are built in Georgian style.

Tudor timber framed houses are built.

Prehistoric man lives in caves.

Terraced houses are built for factory workers.

The Normans begin to build the Tower of London and other castles.

High rise flats are built.

Use these events to begin your own time-line of the history of houses. Find some more important events and place them in the right place on your time line.

© David Wray 1991, *The Project Research Pack*, Stanley Thornes (Publishers) Ltd

Houses for climates

Houses are built in different ways in different countries because the weather in those countries is different. Nobody would try to build an igloo in Saudi Arabia, for example!

Make these four headings in your book.

Hot	Cold	Wet	Windy

Under each heading write down some of the ways in which houses can be built to give the most protection against these types of climate.

For example under *Hot* you might write:

Hot

Houses have plenty
of shade.

They are often built
on pillars or stilts
so draughts can
pass round them
etc.

You will need to search carefully through the information in your books. The index of each book will help you.

© David Wray 1991, *The Project Research Pack*, Stanley Thornes (Publishers) Ltd

Building a house

Here is a flow-chart for building a house.

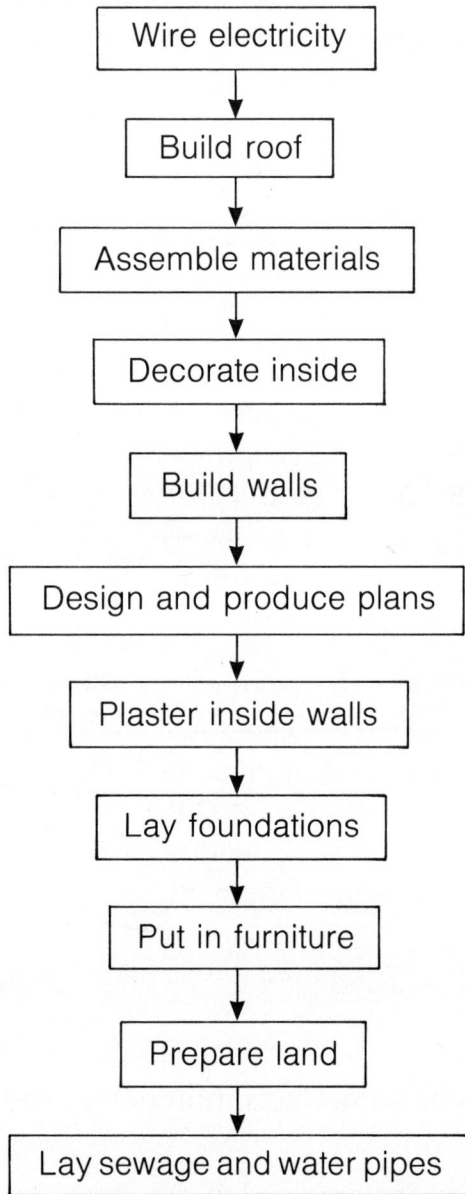

```
┌─────────────────────────────┐
│      Wire electricity       │
└─────────────────────────────┘
              ↓
┌─────────────────────────────┐
│         Build roof          │
└─────────────────────────────┘
              ↓
┌─────────────────────────────┐
│     Assemble materials      │
└─────────────────────────────┘
              ↓
┌─────────────────────────────┐
│       Decorate inside       │
└─────────────────────────────┘
              ↓
┌─────────────────────────────┐
│         Build walls         │
└─────────────────────────────┘
              ↓
┌─────────────────────────────┐
│   Design and produce plans  │
└─────────────────────────────┘
              ↓
┌─────────────────────────────┐
│     Plaster inside walls    │
└─────────────────────────────┘
              ↓
┌─────────────────────────────┐
│        Lay foundations      │
└─────────────────────────────┘
              ↓
┌─────────────────────────────┐
│      Put in furniture       │
└─────────────────────────────┘
              ↓
┌─────────────────────────────┐
│        Prepare land         │
└─────────────────────────────┘
              ↓
┌─────────────────────────────┐
│  Lay sewage and water pipes │
└─────────────────────────────┘
```

You have probably noticed that this chart is in the wrong order. If a builder followed it he would build a strange house! Can you sort it out?

Your reference books might help you with this.

© David Wray 1991, *The Project Research Pack*, Stanley Thornes (Publishers) Ltd

Activity 8

Selling your house

When people sell houses they usually use an estate agent to help them. The estate agent's job is to advertise the house and to try to persuade people to buy it. The estate agent will usually produce a leaflet with information about the house. This is the sort of thing the leaflet will say:

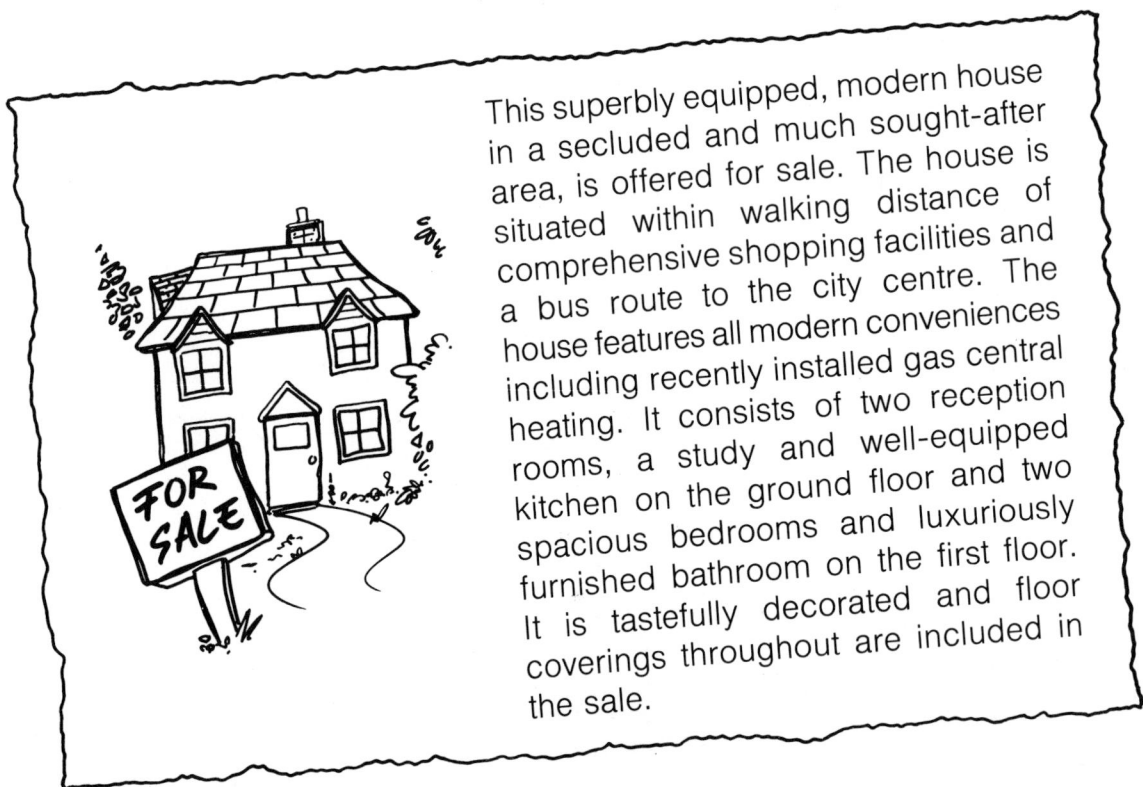

This superbly equipped, modern house in a secluded and much sought-after area, is offered for sale. The house is situated within walking distance of comprehensive shopping facilities and a bus route to the city centre. The house features all modern conveniences including recently installed gas central heating. It consists of two reception rooms, a study and well-equipped kitchen on the ground floor and two spacious bedrooms and luxuriously furnished bathroom on the first floor. It is tastefully decorated and floor coverings throughout are included in the sale.

This description contains some facts: number of rooms, type of central heating etc.

It also contains some statements which are there just to make the house sound good. Can you underline some statements of this kind?

Try to collect some examples of estate agents' leaflets and read the descriptions they give of the houses.

Write a leaflet advertising your own house in the same style an estate agent would use. Make your house sound *really* good!

© David Wray 1991, *The Project Research Pack*, Stanley Thornes (Publishers) Ltd

Houses of the future

What kind of homes do you think we will live in in the future?

You might be able to find some predictions about the houses of the future in your reference books. Try to sort out these predictions into two kinds:

Predictions I think will come true	Predictions I do not think will come true

For each prediction you list under these headings try to give a reason why you think it will or will not come true. For example, one of the predictions you might think will come true is that eventually men will live in houses on the moon. You might give as reasons for this that the earth might get overcrowded and that people might discover ways of building completely air-tight domes in which to build houses.

When you have thought about houses in the future, write an account for your project folder on:

Homes in the Future.

© David Wray 1991, *The Project Research Pack*, Stanley Thornes (Publishers) Ltd

The Vikings

USING THE ACTIVITIES

The appropriateness of these activities for particular groups of children will depend upon a number of things, including their previous experience with this kind of work. Teachers are therefore urged to use the activity sheets as they think appropriate. A tentative grading might, however, be as follows:

Lower juniors (ages 7–9): Activities 1, 3, 4, 5, 7
Upper juniors (ages 9–11): Activities 2, 6, 8, 9

These activities can be done as self-contained exercises, but they will all benefit greatly from discussion beforehand, and (especially) afterwards. All the activities will work best if tackled by two or three children together.

In the case of Activities 3, 4, 5, 6, 7 and 8 discussion will be needed beforehand to point out the use of reference sources to the children, and afterwards to draw their attention to the way they were able to use these sources. For sheet 5 the use of the atlas will also need to be discussed.

SKILLS TO BE DEVELOPED

Activity 1
The children are here asked to pose questions about their topic from a special point of view. They will probably need some discussion beforehand about the job of a television reporter, and some discussion about the content and style of TV documentaries.

Activity 2
Again the children are asked to pose questions from a particular point of view. The activity would be greatly aided if the children had some prior experience of looking at historical records, even if only pictorial ones.

Activity 3
This is an information–location task but one which will demand a slightly different approach to the more usual use of an index. Here the children will have to find the information they want from the midst of longer text by using contents pages.

Activity 4
This is a straightforward information finding and matching task. It focuses particularly upon the use of an index to locate information.

Activity 5
This activity involves the selection of information. Children will have to combine the use of their reference books with the use of modern atlas. They may need some guidance in the most efficient ways to use these different information sources.

Activity 6
In this activity the children are asked to compile information and then to use this as the basis for an extended piece of writing. They may be unfamiliar with using information in this way.

Activity 7
Again children have to compile information and then to reorganise it into an extended piece of writing, in this case an imaginative story. This technique can be used in many different projects and, hopefully, will have the effect of improving the authenticity of children's writing about historical events.

Activity 8
This activity asks children to evaluate evidence they find referred to in books. The concept of evidence may require some discussion. Children may also need some guidance in presenting their evidence in the form of an argument. This might best be done first as an oral activity before moving to writing.

Activity 9
Here children are asked to evaluate reported information. It focuses upon exaggeration as a form of bias in writing. It could usefully be following up by children discussing other forms and instances of bias in information sources.

Skills analysis

Topic: Vikings	Skill stage				
	1	2	3	4	5
Activity 1	✓				
Activity 2	✓				
Activity 3		✓			
Activity 4		✓			
Activity 5		✓	✓		
Activity 6		✓	✓	✓	
Activity 7		✓	✓	✓	
Activity 8		✓	✓	✓	✓
Activity 9					✓

Making a TV documentary

I am a film maker. I've been asked by the BBC to make a television film about the Vikings. They don't want an action packed film all about fighting and things, but a documentary about how the Vikings actually lived.

The first thing they have asked me to do is to find out what the people who might watch this film will expect to see in it. Can you help me?

What kinds of things do you think should be in a film about the Vikings? I have already thought of things like:

Showing what the lands where the Vikings came from were like

Showing how the Vikings lived at home.

Can you add anything to my list?

When you have added a few things you think would be interesting, show your list to some of your friends. Can they help you by adding anything to your list?

© David Wray 1991, *The Project Research Pack*, Stanley Thornes (Publishers) Ltd

Be a historian

An historian is someone who finds out things about the past. The historian starts with any evidence there is about the past, such as the remains of buildings, or old books and documents, and then asks questions about this evidence.

Imagine you are an historian. You have just found the remains of a Viking ship buried in earth close to a beach.

After examining the ship there are lots of questions you want to ask.

You might want to ask:
How was this ship built?
How did it sail?
How many people could sail on it?

Can you think of other questions you might ask about what you have found?

Real historians have done just this with the remains which have been found of real Viking ships.

When you have thought of the questions to ask, you might be able to answer some of them by looking in books written by historians.

Are there any questions which you cannot answer? If there are, you might think whether these questions are impossible to answer, or whether more evidence is needed to answer them.

© David Wray 1991, *The Project Research Pack*, Stanley Thornes (Publishers) Ltd

Activity
3

The Viking ship

Here is a picture of a Viking ship.

MAST

OARS

Only some parts of the ship have been labelled.

Can you fill in the missing labels?

Can you find out some things about these ships?
   Where did those who sailed on them sleep?
   Where did they keep their belongings?
   What did they eat and drink?

Perhaps there are some other questions you would like to know the answers to?

You will need to look in reference books for the information about these ships. Remember to use the contents page and the index of the books you use.

© David Wray 1991, *The Project Research Pack*, Stanley Thornes (Publishers) Ltd

Activity 4

Viking gods

The Vikings had many gods. They believed that these gods lived in a place in heaven called Asgard. They told many stories about the adventures of the gods which you will enjoy reading.

In the list below are the names of some of their gods. Opposite each name you are told what that god was the god of. Unfortunately these two lists have been mixed up. Thor was not the god of fire but of thunder, for example.

Can you sort out the list by drawing lines from each god to what he (or she) was really god (or goddess) of? One has already been done for you.

Thor	fire
Odin	poetry
Tyr	thunder
Freya	mischief
Loki	plenty
Njord	father of the gods
Bragi	war
Surtur	sea

Remember to use the index of the books you use to help you.

© David Wray 1991, *The Project Research Pack*, Stanley Thornes (Publishers) Ltd

Viking voyages

Here is a map of the world of the Vikings.

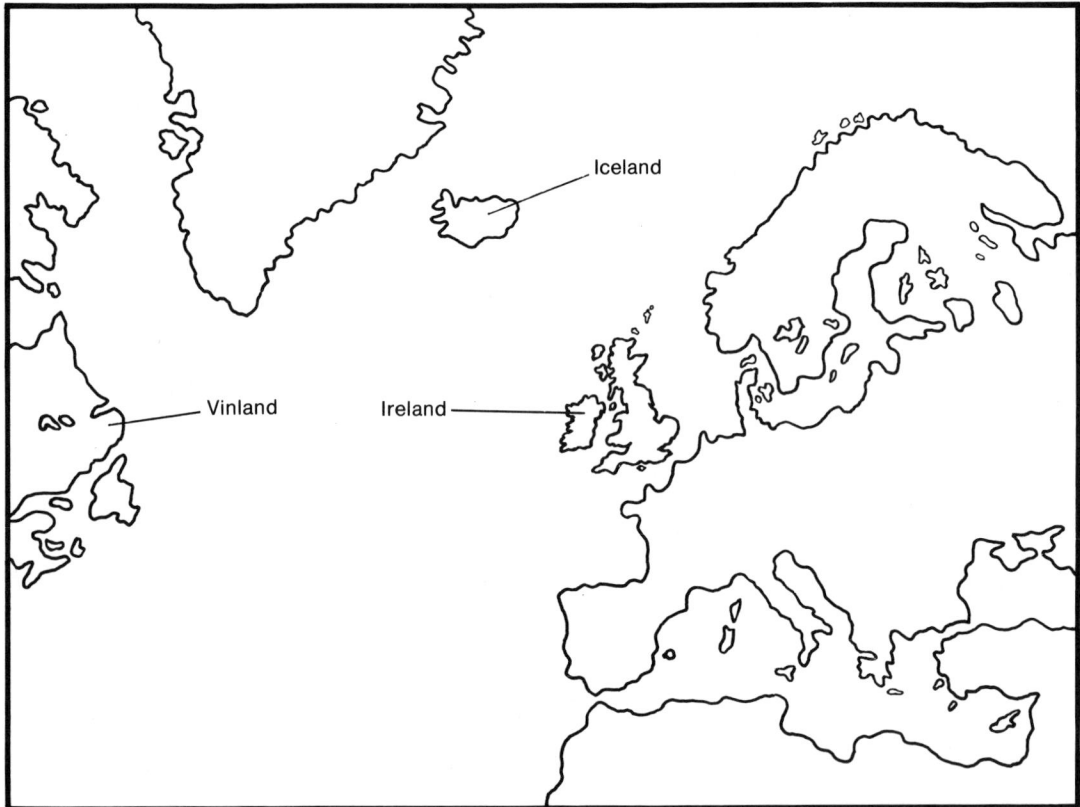

On this map try to mark some of the places to which the Vikings went and settled. Some have already been marked for you, but can you find out where these places were and mark them on the map?

> Normandy
> Strathclyde
> Greenland
> Kiev
> The Danelaw
> Constantinople

You will find some of these places in modern atlases, but you might need to look for some in your reference books first.

© David Wray 1991, *The Project Research Pack*, Stanley Thornes (Publishers) Ltd

King Canute

King Canute was one of the most famous kings of the Vikings. He became, not only King of the Vikings, but King of England as well.

See if you can find out some things about him from your books.

Try to find the answers to these questions. Just jot down your answers as quick notes for the moment.

1 When was Canute born?

2 Where did he live as a child?

3 What kind of man was he?

4 When did he first become a king, and how?

5 How did he become King of England?

6 What stories were told about him?

7 What did he do as king?

8 When and how did he die?

9 Who became King of England after him?

10 How did the Vikings lose the kingship of England?

When you have got all this information, try to use it to write the story of:
King Canute, the Viking King of England.

If you include some pictures of Canute, and of his Vikings, and some maps and diagrams, your story will make a useful booklet to display with the rest of your Viking project work.

© David Wray 1991, The Project Research Pack, Stanley Thornes (Publishers) Ltd

Activity 7

A Viking voyage

The Vikings were great sailors. They went on many voyages to strange lands, some of which nobody had discovered before. These voyages must have been full of danger and excitement, and the people who went on them must have been very brave.

Try to write an exciting story about a Viking voyage. Before you begin you will need to know lots of things about the Vikings and their ships. If you find out the answers to the questions below this will give you a good start towards your story.

1 How were Viking ships built?
2 How did they travel through the water?
3 How many people could a ship hold?
4 Where would they sleep on board?
5 Where would they store their equipment?
6 What kind of food did they eat?
7 Was there any shelter from storms?
8 How fast did the ships travel?
9 What did the Vikings do when they were not rowing or fighting?
10 How were the ships steered?

© David Wray 1991, *The Project Research Pack*, Stanley Thornes (Publishers) Ltd

Activity 8

Viking explorers

The Vikings visited many, many places. Sometimes they just went to raid, and came back home afterwards with treasures or slaves they captured. Sometimes they went to settle, taking their families with them and building new lives in the places they went to.

It is sometimes hard to understand why they went to all the places they did. There could have been different reasons.

1 They might just have been very fierce people who enjoyed making war on others.

2 Their own countries might have been very hard places to live in, so they looked for somewhere easier.

3 There might have been too many of them to live in their own countries.

4 They might have been natural explorers who simply wanted to find out what was over the horizon.

Which of these reasons do you think was most likely?

Look through your reference books to see if you can find any information which might make you believe in any of these reasons.

Write a short account in your book with the title:

Why did the Vikings leave their homes?

© David Wray 1991, *The Project Research Pack*, Stanley Thornes (Publishers) Ltd

Oh, those dreadful Vikings!

Because the Vikings did not write very much themselves, the accounts which we have of their raids were mostly written by their enemies. Here is an extract from an account of a Viking raid written by a man who lived at the time.

My friend and I saw the ships as we were guarding the sheep. There were many, many of them. I counted forty, at least. They were sailing like flying arrows towards our village!

We ran to warn the village. Everyone began to panic, packing up their belongings and running away from the village. A few brave men said they would stay and fight, and I stayed with them. We had not long to wait. An army of Vikings came up the beach and began to set fire to our houses. There were hundreds of them, each one over six feet tall, carrying an enormous double-headed axe, and wearing a helmet crowned with eagles' wings.

Even though our men struck many of them with their swords they could not kill them, and the giants kept advancing. At last we gave up and ran away. Nobody can defeat these awful men from the sea. From the fury of the Northmen, good Lord deliver us.

Do you think this story is completely true? When people are afraid they sometimes exaggerate what they see. Underline pieces of the story which you think might be exaggerations.

Write a version of this story which you think might be a more accurate account of the raid. You will need to find out some facts about Viking raids, such as: How many men did one ship hold? What weapons did they have? What armour did they wear? What kind of men were they?

© David Wray 1991, *The Project Research Pack*, Stanley Thornes (Publishers) Ltd

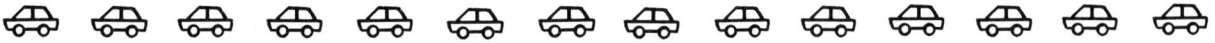

Transport

USING THE ACTIVITIES

The appropriateness of these activities for particular groups of children will depend upon a number of things, including their previous experience with this kind of work. Teachers are therefore urged to use the activity sheets as they think appropriate. A tentative grading might, however, be as follows:

Lower juniors (ages 7–9): Activities 1, 3, 4, 5, 8
Upper juniors (ages 9–11): Activities 2, 6, 7, 9

These activities, with the exception perhaps of Activity 2 which sets the scene for some valuable work, can be done as self-contained exercises. They will all benefit greatly, however, from discussion beforehand, and (especially) afterwards, between teacher and children and between the children themselves.

In the case of Activities 3, 4 and 5 discussion will be needed beforehand to point out the use of reference books to the children, and afterwards to draw their attention to the way they were able to use these books. Activity 8 may need some explanation to children not familiar with tree diagrams.

SKILLS TO BE DEVELOPED

Activity 1
The activity is intended to get children to ask questions as a preliminary to answering them. They should be encouraged to do this prior to most information handling tasks.

Activity 2
This again focuses upon the asking of questions, but of a more general kind. Children should be asked to go beyond their chapter headings to detail the more specific questions each chapter will answer.

Activity 3
This is a straightforward information-finding task. Children may need some help in deciding which words to look for in index pages.

Activity 4
This activity again requires the location of particular information. The children will be looking for dates and this provides a good opportunity to introduce them to the technique of scanning – that is, glancing quickly at a page to find a specific piece of information.

Activity 5
Another information location task. As the information the children will be looking for will probably be in the form of figures, they will again be practising scanning.

Activity 6
This focuses upon the selection of particular items of information which might be buried quite densely in continuous text. As such it is a rather more difficult task than the location of dates or figures. When they have found the information the children are asked to reorganise it into a narrative account.

Activity 7
This activity requires children to organise information into a grid format. The allocation of the appropriate figures will require discussion, as will their responses to the questions they are asked about the grid. The activity opens up questions of judgement and therefore involves children in evaluation as well.

Activity 8
Here the children are introduced to a different way of organising information, and they are asked both to use the tree structure and to extend it. They may be familiar with this kind of format from work on the computer.

Activity 9
This activity intends children to look critically and evaluate information they come across, in this case in advertisements. The activity of designing their own advertisement can be very beneficial in alerting them to the way persuasive techniques work.

Skills analysis

Topic: Transport	Skill stage				
	1	2	3	4	5
Activity 1	√				
Activity 2	√				
Activity 3		√			
Activity 4		√	√		
Activity 5		√	√		
Activity 6		√	√	√	
Activity 7				√	√
Activity 8				√	
Activity 9					√

Activity 1

Ask about...

Look at this picture of a car.

Lee liked this picture. There were lots of questions he wanted to ask about it.

1 What kind of car is it?

2 How fast can it go?

3 Does it use a lot of petrol?

4 How much would it cost to buy?

What other questions could Lee ask?

Find your own picture of a car. Show it to your friend and get your friend to ask you questions about it. Can you answer your friend's questions?

© David Wray 1991, *The Project Research Pack*, Stanley Thornes (Publishers) Ltd

Activity

2

Be an author

A person who writes books is called an author. I am an author. I am writing a book about railway trains.

The first thing I have to do is to decide what kinds of things I want to say in my book and what sections it will have. The sections of a book are called chapters.

1 The first railways.

2 The spread of the railways.

3 Railways today.

4 How steam trains worked.

5 How a modern railway train works.

6 . . . .

7 . . . .

8 . . . .

9 . . . .

What other chapters might I have? Can you add some to the list?

Suppose you were an author writing a book on either:
Ships
Cars
Aeroplanes.

What chapters would you include in your book?

© David Wray 1991, *The Project Research Pack*, Stanley Thornes (Publishers) Ltd

Activity
3

True or false?

Here are ten sentences about transport. Some of them are true and some are false. Can you say which is which? You will have to use reference books to find out. Remember to use the contents and the index pages.

1 Most cars have internal combustion engines.

2 A Jumbo Jet can carry over 200 passengers.

3 Airships used to be filled with hot air.

4 'The Rocket' was one of the first steam trains and was built by George Stevenson.

5 'The Titanic' sank when it ran aground on the coast of America.

6 The first man to sail right round the world was Sir Francis Drake.

7 London Underground trains nowadays run on electricity.

8 One of the first bicycles was called the 'Penny Farthing' because that was how much it cost to buy in those days.

9 The first man to fly an aeroplane across the Atlantic Ocean was called Louis Bleriot.

10 When the first cars were driven they had to have a man walking in front of them waving a red flag.

Make up some sentences like this for yourself. See if your friend can tell which are true and which false.

First in time

Here are some famous events in the history of transport. Unfortunately they are in the wrong order. Can you rearrange them so that the event which happened first is placed first, and so on? Remember to use the index pages of your reference books to help you.

You might find it easier to cut out these sentences and stick them into your book in the right order.

The Wright brothers made the first flight in an aeroplane.

Henry Ford built the Model T car.

George Stevenson built his steam train, 'The Rocket'.

The Montgolfier brothers built the first hot air balloon.

Isambard Brunel built the first steamship.

James Watt invented the steam engine.

Use these events to begin your own time-line of the history of transport. Find some more important events and place them in the right place on your time-line.

© David Wray 1991, *The Project Research Pack*, Stanley Thornes (Publishers) Ltd

The fastest

Here are pictures of some famous aeroplanes.

	Concord Speed . . . . . .
	A Spitfire Speed . . . . . .
	A Jumbo Jet Speed . . . . . .
	A Hawker Harrier Jet Speed . . . . . .
	. . . . Speed . . . . . .

How fast can each of these planes fly? Write its top speed in the box. Find a plane that will go faster than any of them and draw a picture of it in the empty box.

Cut out the pictures and arrange all these aeroplanes in order of speed, putting the fastest first and the slowest in last position. You will need to use your reference books carefully for this.

© David Wray 1991, *The Project Research Pack*, Stanley Thornes (Publishers) Ltd

Eye witness

The very first people to build an aeroplane which took off and flew under its own power were Orville and Wilbur Wright – the Wright brothers. The very first flight of this aeroplane must have been very exciting.

Imagine you had been there and had witnessed the first flight.

Other people might have asked you questions like:

When was the first flight?
Where did it happen?
Who was there?
What took place?
What did the people there say?

Try to find answers to these questions using reference books.

When you have got the answers, write an account of the Wright brothers' first flight as if you had been an *eye-witness*. You could write this in the form of a letter to a friend or in the form of a newspaper report.

Imagine you had been an eye-witness to another important event:

The first flight across the Atlantic ocean
The first flight around the world
Or another event you might choose.

Using the questions above, gather enough information to write an *eye-witness* account of this event.

© David Wray 1991, *The Project Research Pack*, Stanley Thornes (Publishers) Ltd

Which is best?

Activity 7

There are several ways of travelling from place to place. You can go by air, train, bus or car. How can we decide which is the best way?

One way is to use the table below. Down the side of the table are the ways of travelling. Along the top are things we might mean by 'best'.

'Best' sometimes means 'fastest', so speed is the first heading.
'Best' sometimes means 'cheapest', so cost is the second heading.
'Best' sometimes means 'easiest to use', so ease of use is the third heading.
'Best' sometimes means 'most restful', so restful is the fourth heading.

One heading has been left empty for you to complete.

	Speed	Cost	Easy to use	Restful	
Air	1				
Train	2				
Bus	4				
Car	3				

The numbers in the boxes show which is the best type of transport. Air travel is the fastest, so it has been given 1. Bus travel is the slowest so it has been given 4.

Try to fill in the rest of the boxes. You will need to look at some timetables and ask some people as well as using your reference books.

Use your grid to decide which is the best form of transport for these people:

Mrs Marple is a pensioner who lives in London and wants to visit her grandchildren in Scotland.

Miss Price is a student in Cardiff who wants to visit Yorkshire on a camping holiday.

Mr Jones is a businessman in Newcastle who has an urgent meeting in London.

© David Wray 1991, *The Project Research Pack*, Stanley Thornes (Publishers) Ltd

Transport trees

One way of sorting out information is to use a tree diagram. Here is an example of one to do with methods of transport.

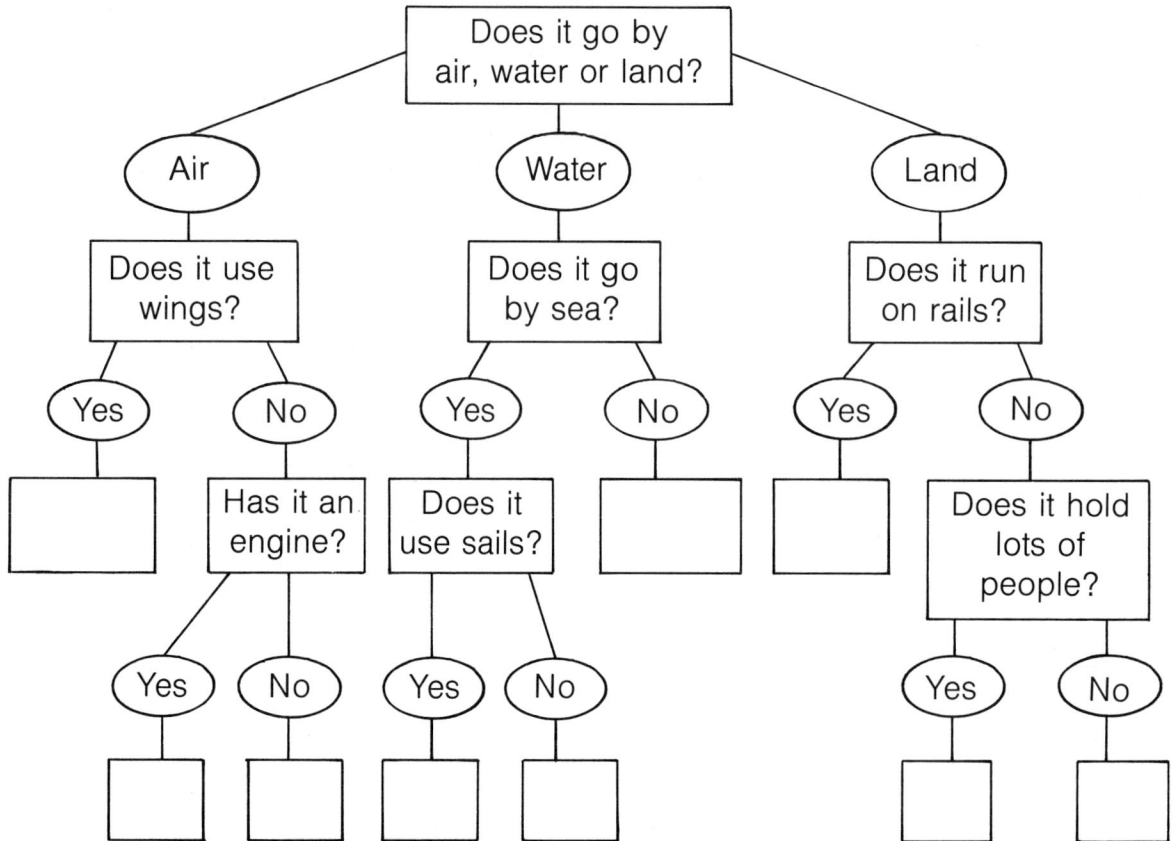

```
                    ┌─────────────────┐
                    │  Does it go by  │
                    │ air, water or land? │
                    └─────────────────┘
         ┌──────────────┬──────────────┐
      (Air)          (Water)         (Land)
         │              │              │
   ┌──────────┐   ┌──────────┐   ┌──────────┐
   │ Does it use │ │ Does it go │ │ Does it run │
   │  wings?  │   │  by sea? │   │ on rails? │
   └──────────┘   └──────────┘   └──────────┘
   (Yes)  (No)    (Yes)  (No)    (Yes)  (No)
    │      │       │      │       │      │
  ┌───┐ ┌──────┐ ┌──────┐ ┌───┐ ┌───┐ ┌──────────┐
  │   │ │ Has it an │ │ Does it │ │   │ │   │ │ Does it hold │
  │   │ │ engine?│ │ use sails?│ │   │ │   │ │  lots of │
  └───┘ └──────┘ └──────┘ └───┘ └───┘ │  people? │
        (Yes)(No) (Yes)(No)          └──────────┘
         │   │     │   │             (Yes)  (No)
        ┌─┐ ┌─┐  ┌─┐ ┌─┐              │      │
        │ │ │ │  │ │ │ │            ┌───┐  ┌───┐
        └─┘ └─┘  └─┘ └─┘            │   │  │   │
                                    └───┘  └───┘
```

Can you fill in the empty boxes with the names of types of transport?

You will need to follow the questions through and find out from your books which types of transport will fit.

Can you add any more questions to the bottom of the branches of the tree?

© David Wray 1991, *The Project Research Pack*, Stanley Thornes (Publishers) Ltd

Advertisements

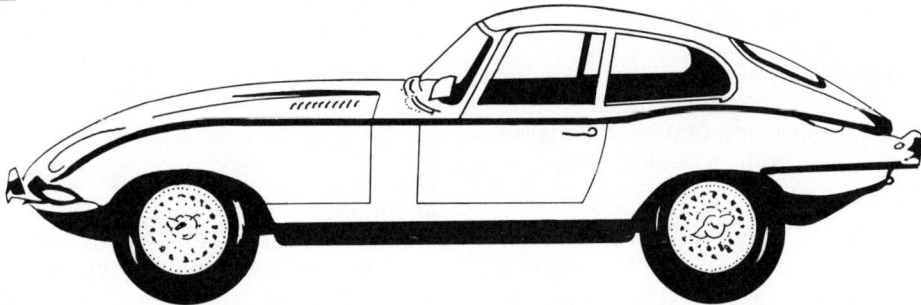

Advertisements are usually made up of statements which are real facts, and statements which are there just to try to persuade you to buy what is being advertised. We need to be able to tell these statements apart.

Look through some magazines and find an advertisement for a car that you really like.

Make two headings in your book: *Facts*, and *Statements to persuade*. Read your advertisement and try to write down some of the things it says under the right heading. The list below might give you a start.

Facts	Statements to persuade
Top speed 95 m.p.h. Costs £6,950. Five gears.	Cruises effortlessly. Several built-in extras. A dream to drive.

Think of the car you would most like to own. Write down some *facts* about it. Write down some things you would say about it if you were trying to persuade someone else to buy it.

Using a mixture of these facts and statements to persuade, design your own advertisement for your car. Your advertisement will need to include an appealing picture of the car.

© David Wray 1991, *The Project Research Pack*, Stanley Thornes (Publishers) Ltd

Dinosaurs

USING THE ACTIVITIES

The appropriateness of these activities for particular groups of children will depend upon a number of things, including their previous experience with this kind of work. Teachers are therefore urged to use the activity sheets as they think appropriate. A tentative grading might, however, be as follows:

Lower juniors (ages 7–9): Activities 1, 3, 4, 5, 9
Upper juniors (ages 9–11): Activities 2, 6, 7, 8

These activities can be done as self-contained exercises, but they will all benefit greatly from discussion beforehand and (especially) afterwards.

In the case of Activities 3, 4, 6, and 7 discussion will be needed beforehand to point out the use of reference books to the children, and afterwards to draw their attention to the way they were able to use these books.

SKILLS TO BE DEVELOPED

Activity 1
This is a version of the familiar 20 questions game and focuses very much upon the kind of questions which children ask. Through playing the game they will gradually come to realise that there are some questions which are more useful than others and this should help them formulate appropriate questions for their project work.

Activity 2
This again focuses upon the asking of questions. Children should be expected to formulate a list of questions which they then group into book chapter headings. This is an important stage in the question formulation process. They are also asked to think about how these questions might be answered. Strategies which are not given, but the children may suggest, include looking in museums, watching television programmes and asking other people.

Activity 3
This activity aims to develop the skills of finding information in reference books. Most of the answers can be obtained by looking up single words in an index or an encyclopaedia. The activity is self-monitoring.

Activity 4
This extends the skills aimed at in the previous activity. The children have to find specific pieces of information about particular dinosaurs. They are introduced to lists of information.

Activity 5
Here the children have not only to find certain information but to make selections from it which meet their purposes. The activity therefore requires a different quality of thinking from the previous two, in which children were given definitive criteria for choosing information. Here they have to determine their own criteria.

Activity 6
The children are introduced here to a particular way of organising information using a grid format. They also, of course, have to be able to find the information they require. Children often find the grid format difficult and completed grids can be used as a focus for discussion with other children.

Activity 7
In addition to requiring information to be organised into particular categories, this activity also introduces the idea of the evaluation of information. Organisation here is more than just assigning items of information to categories, but involves the interpretation of the information first of all.

Activity 8
Children are introduced here to the idea that there are reasons why we believe particular things to be true, and that the information handling process involves the presentation of evidence. This scientific approach is one they may meet elsewhere in their curriculum, but perhaps not employ in their reading of information books.

Activity 9
Distinguishing between fact and opinion is an important element in the evaluation of information. It should be pointed out to children that books sometimes contain opinions which are presented as facts.

NB Some of the creatures mentioned on these sheets are technically 'pre-historic reptiles' rather than 'dinosaurs'. Children will know them best, however, as dinosaurs, and this is a convenient label.

Skills analysis

Topic: Dinosaurs	Skill stage				
	1	2	3	4	5
Activity 1	√				
Activity 2	√				
Activity 3		√			
Activity 4		√	√		
Activity 5		√	√		
Activity 6		√	√	√	
Activity 7				√	√
Activity 8					√
Activity 9					√

Activity 1

Mystery dinosaurs

This is a game you can play with a friend. One of you has to think of the name of a dinosaur. The other person has to try to guess this name by asking questions. They must be questions which can be answered by either 'Yes' or 'No'. If the person asking the questions has not guessed the name of the dinosaur after asking ten questions, the first person is the winner.

Lisa and Darren played this game. Lisa thought of a dinosaur and Darren tried to guess it.

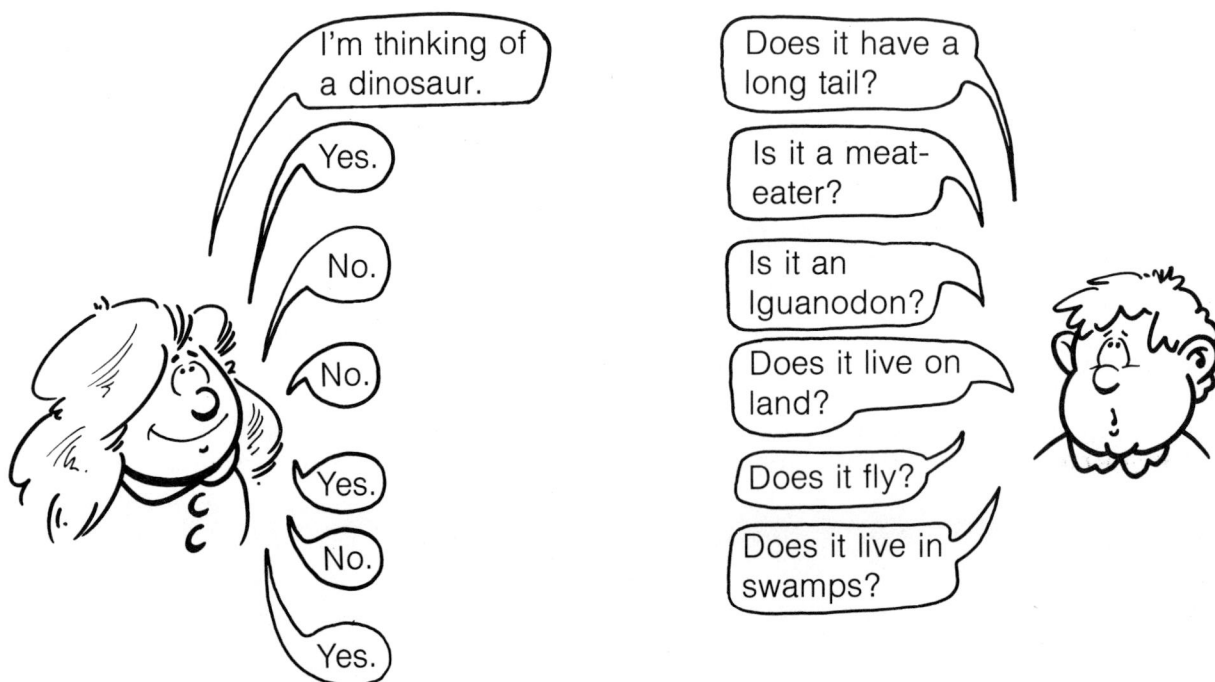

I'm thinking of a dinosaur.

Does it have a long tail?

Yes.

Is it a meat-eater?

No.

Is it an Iguanodon?

No.

Does it live on land?

Yes.

Does it fly?

No.

Does it live in swamps?

Yes.

What question would you ask next if you were Darren? Can you guess which dinosaur Lisa is thinking of?

Did you notice that some questions that Darren asked were better than others? What kind of questions do you think are the best ones to ask?

You can play this game with your friend. Think carefully about the questions you ask. You might find that a reference book will help you ask really good questions.

© David Wray 1991, *The Project Research Pack*, Stanley Thornes (Publishers) Ltd

Activity 2 · Hunting dinosaurs

This man is a dinosaur hunter. He is a scientist. He knows that there are no dinosaurs still living but he wants to find out all he can about these creatures who died out millions of years ago.

He starts by writing down in his notebook all the things he wants to find out.

Can you add to this list of things? Write down some more things you would like to find out about dinosaurs.

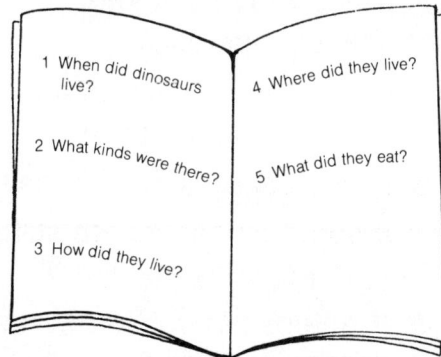

1 When did dinosaurs live?

2 What kinds were there?

3 How did they live?

4 Where did they live?

5 What did they eat?

How will the scientist find out all these things?

He could go and hunt for fossils to study.
He could read books that other scientists have written.

Can you think of any other ways?

When he has found out lots of things about dinosaurs the scientist will write a book about them. The first chapter of his book will be called, 'What is a dinosaur?'

What other chapters do you think he will have in his book?

© David Wray 1991, *The Project Research Pack*, Stanley Thornes (Publishers) Ltd

Dinosaur puzzle

If you can solve this puzzle you will find out the state of dinosaurs today.

A word is hidden in the pattern below. To discover it, read each of the sentences carefully. If a sentence is true, colour in the spaces you are told to. If the sentence is not true, do not colour in anything.

Remember you will need to check your facts in a reference book or encyclopaedia.

1 If the scientific name for a person who studies the plants and animals which lived long ago is a 'paleontologist', colour in the spaces marked **1**.

2 If *Pteranodon* was a winged reptile that soared through the air, colour in the spaces marked **2**.

3 If *Stegosaurus* was fast and slender, colour in the spaces marked **3**.

4 If *Proceratops* is known as the 'egg-laying' dinosaur, colour in the spaces marked **4**.

5 If *Tyrannosaurus* was a huge, fierce, meat-eating dinosaur, colour in the spaces marked **5**.

6 If *Plesiosaurus* lived in caves, colour in the spaces marked **6**.

7 If some dinosaurs are still living in the jungles of the Amazon, colour in the spaces marked **7**.

8 If *Anatosaurus* is known as the 'duck-billed' dinosaur, colour in the spaces marked **8**.

9 If *Diplodocus* was a small, meat-eating dinosaur, colour in the spaces marked **9**.

6	3	9	7	3	6	9	7	6/3	9	7	6	3	9	6	3	7	6	9	3	9	3	6/3	9	7	3	9
7	6	7	3	9	3	6	3/6	7/6	3	6	7	6	3	9	6	9	6	7	6	7	6	6	3	6/3	6	6/3
3	9	7	6	7	6	7	7/6	9	7	3	6	7	9	7	9	3	3	9	7	3/6	9	7	6	7	9	7
7	2	5/8	6	1	3	5	9	8/5	4	8	9	1	3	4	2/3	9	8	7	3/5	4	8	6	2	1/4	8	9
6	4	3	7	6/8	7	2/6	3	6	2	3	9	4	6	1	6/5	4/7	5	9	8	6	3	7	6	8	3	7
9	8	5	9	3	1	9	6	7	8	7	3	8	9	5	3	9/2	1	6	1	7	6	3	9	5	6	9
6	2	3	6	3/4	9	5/7	3	6	4	9	7	2	6	8	7	9	4	3	2	3	7	9	6	8	3	7
3	4/5	1	3	2	7	4	9	7	2/1	6	3	1	7	5	6	7	2	7	6/4	5	1	7	3	1	7	6
7	6/3	6	7	3	9	6	7	9	7	6	7	3	6	3	9	3	7	6	7	9	3/7	6	7/9	6	7/9	3
6	7/9	6/7	9	7	6	3	7	3	9/3	7	6/3	7	7	9	6	7	3	7	9	7	9	3	6	9	9	7
3	6	7	3	9	7	7	6	9	7	7	3	6	9	6/3	9	7	6	7	6	9	3	7	3	6	3	6

© David Wray 1991, *The Project Research Pack*, Stanley Thornes (Publishers) Ltd

Sorting dinosaurs

Activity 4

Can you add the names of three or four other dinosaurs to this list? *Diplodocus, Ichthyosaurus, Iguanodon, Plesiosaurus, Pteranodon, Stegosaurus, Triceratops, Tyrannosaurus.* . . . .

Can you sort out your list of dinosaurs in the following ways? (Remember you will need to use reference books to help you.)

1 Where did these dinosaurs live? Write the name of each dinosaur under the right heading in your book.

On land	In the water	In the air	In swamps

2 What did they eat? Make two lists, one of the carnivores (meat-eaters) and one of the herbivores (plant-eaters). Were there any dinosaurs which should go in both lists? What would you call these?

3 How big were they? Cut out the pictures of the dinosaurs and arrange them in order of size, putting the longest first and the shortest last.

Can you think of any other ways of sorting out these dinosaurs?

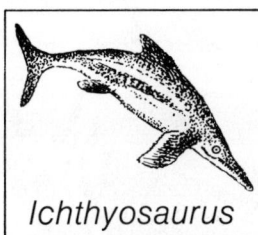

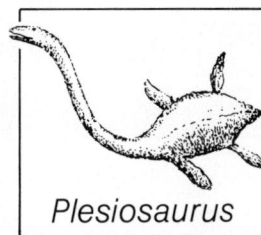

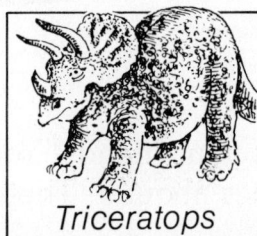

Diplodocus *Ichthyosaurus* *Iguanodon* *Plesiosaurus*

Pteranodon *Stegosaurus* *Triceratops* *Tyrannosaurus*

Make some cards with pictures of your favourite dinosaurs.

© David Wray 1991, *The Project Research Pack*, Stanley Thornes (Publishers) Ltd

Activity
5

Dinosaur clues

I am thinking of a dinosaur.
Can you guess its name?
Here are some clues to help
you.

1 This dinosaur eats plants.
2 It walks upright on two legs.
3 It has a big, powerful tail.

Have you guessed it?
Here is a picture of it.

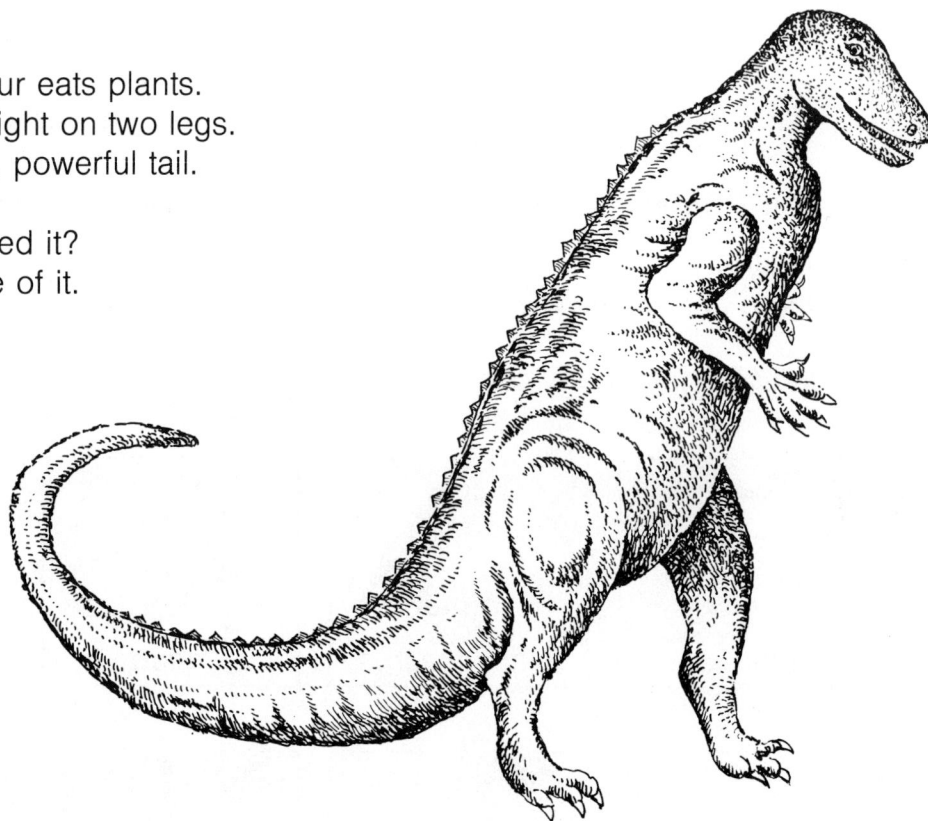

Play this game with your friends. You have to think of a dinosaur and give them some clues about it. They have to try to guess its name.

You will need to look in reference books to help you choose which clues to give.

© David Wray 1991, *The Project Research Pack*, Stanley Thornes (Publishers) Ltd

Dinosaur facts

Down the left hand side of the grid below write the names of ten dinosaurs you have heard about.

For each of these dinosaurs try to answer the questions along the top of the grid. Put the answers in the correct boxes. Sometimes you will need to put in a number or a word, and sometimes a tick or a cross will do.

Remember that you will need to use the contents and index pages of the reference books you look in.

Names of dinosaurs / Questions	How long was it?	Where did it live?				What did it eat?
		On land	In the water	In the air	In a swamp	
1						
2						
3						
4						
5						
6						
7						
8						
9						
10						

© David Wray 1991, *The Project Research Pack*, Stanley Thornes (Publishers) Ltd

The end of the dinosaurs

The dinosaurs all died out millions of years ago. Nobody really knows why they became extinct, but there are lots of theories.

One theory is that the earth became colder because an ice age was beginning, and the dinosaurs could not keep warm enough to survive.

Another theory is that the earth was hit by a giant meteor and the debris from this caused great clouds of dust which blocked out the sun. The dinosaurs needed the sun's heat to keep warm and could not survive without it.

Another theory is that there were many volcanoes and earthquakes which changed the face of the earth so much that the dinosaurs could no longer find the right food.

You might have your own theory about the end of the dinosaurs.

Make four headings in your book with some space under each of them:

The ice age theory	The meteor theory	The earthquakes theory	My own theory

Look in your reference books to see if you can find any information which supports any of these theories. If you find some, make a note of it under the heading of the theory it supports.

When you have done this using several reference books, decide which of the theories you now think is more likely to be correct. Write a paragraph explaining why you think this theory is the best one.

© David Wray 1991, *The Project Research Pack*, Stanley Thornes (Publishers) Ltd

How do we know?

This is a *Tyrannosaurus rex*. In your reference books you might find the following statement:

Tyrannosaurus rex was a meat-eating dinosaur.

How do we know this is true?

Can you think of any ways we might know this?

Most of our knowledge comes from the fossils which have been found.

From the fossil remains of *Tyrannosaurus rex*, we know it had very sharp teeth suitable for tearing flesh. We also know it had very powerful back legs and enormous jaws which would have made it a strong fighter. From this information we have worked out that it was probably a meat-eater.

Can you find out how we know the following statements are true?

The *Brontosaurus* lived in swamps and pools.

The *Stegosaurus* was a plant-eater.

The *Plesiosaur* lived in the water.

© David Wray 1991, *The Project Research Pack*, Stanley Thornes (Publishers) Ltd

Activity 9

Facts and opinions

Read the following sentences about dinosaurs.

Dinosaurs lived over three hundred million years ago.

I think the dinosaurs were destroyed by a giant meteor.

Some people say that there are still some dinosaurs alive in the jungles of South America.

The pterodactyl was a flying dinosaur.

Two of these sentences give *facts* about dinosaurs, and two of them give people's *opinions*. Can you decide which is which?

Facts are things that we know are true, because we can prove them. Opinions are things people believe to be true, but which cannot really be proved. Do you think your reference books are more likely to have facts or opinions in them?

Look in a reference book about dinosaurs and find three sentences which you think give facts, and three which you think give opinions. Discuss your sentences with your friends. Do you all agree which are facts and which opinions?

© David Wray 1991, *The Project Research Pack*, Stanley Thornes (Publishers) Ltd

Food

USING THE ACTIVITIES

The appropriateness of these activities for particular groups of children will depend upon a number of things, including their previous experience with this kind of work. Teachers are therefore urged to use the activity sheets as they think appropriate. A tentative grading might, however, be as follows:

Lower juniors (ages 7–9): Activities 1, 2, 4, 6
Upper juniors (ages 9–11): Activities 3, 5, 7, 8, 9

These activities can be done as self-contained exercises, but they will all benefit greatly from discussion beforehand, and (especially) afterwards.

In the case of Activities 2, 3, 4, 6, and 8 discussion will be needed beforehand to point out the use of reference books to the children, and afterwards to draw their attention to the way they were able to use these books.

SKILLS TO BE DEVELOPED

Activity 1
This is a version of the familiar 20 questions game and focuses very much upon the kind of questions which children ask. Through playing the game they will gradually come to realise that there are some questions which are more useful than others and this should help them formulate appropriate questions for their project work.

Activity 2
This introduces the idea a collection of information. It focuses upon the formulation of questions, but will give an opportunity for children to practice finding answers to their questions. A useful extension would be to introduce the children to data-handling programs on the computer. Their dossiers will give a framework for the construction of a computer database.

Activity 3
This is a straightforward information-finding task. A useful point to discuss with the children is which set of words it is most sensible to use as a basis for searching in an index, and how this will depend upon the kind of book they are using.

Activity 4
This is an information-finding task which focuses particularly on the use of an index. The children are asked to use cookery books as a different kind of information source, but they could equally, of course, use a dictionary. The cookery book will, however, give them the information they want in context, and will be essential for the second part of the activity.

Activity 5
The children's attention is drawn to the information given on food packaging. They will need to use other sources to find the significance of this information. The sheet could be a starting point for a great deal of work on food content, including some science, using simple chemical tests for fats, starch etc.

Activity 6
This activity introduces the geographical aspect of food. Some children will be able to do some of the activity from their existing knowledge. The activity cries out to be followed up by a 'Round the World Food Testing'.

Activity 7
Here children are asked to find particular information, and then to reorganise it in a special way. The activity seems simple, but will give rise to a great deal of cross-referencing, number work and proof-reading as children construct their shopping lists. The final part of the sheet requires some work out of school and might be used to involve parents in the project work.

Activity 8
This is a very topical activity which many children will already have begun to think about. In terms of information handling it demands the location and reorganisation of information, but its chief value will probably be in the discussion it stimulates.

Activity 9
This activity aims to get children to look critically and evaluate information they come across, in this case in advertisements. The activity of designing their own advertisement can be very beneficial in alerting them to the way persuasive techniques work.

Skills analysis

Topic: Food	Skill stage				
	1	2	3	4	5
Activity 1	√				
Activity 2	√	√			
Activity 3		√			
Activity 4		√			
Activity 5		√	√		
Activity 6		√	√		
Activity 7		√	√	√	
Activity 8		√	√	√	
Activity 9					√

What is this food?

This is a game you can play with a friend. One of you has to think of a kind of food. The other person has to try to guess the food by asking questions. They must be questions which can be answered 'Yes' or 'No'. If the person asking the questions has not guessed the food after asking ten questions, the first person is the winner.

Tracey and Ian played this game. Tracey thought of a food and Ian tried to guess it.

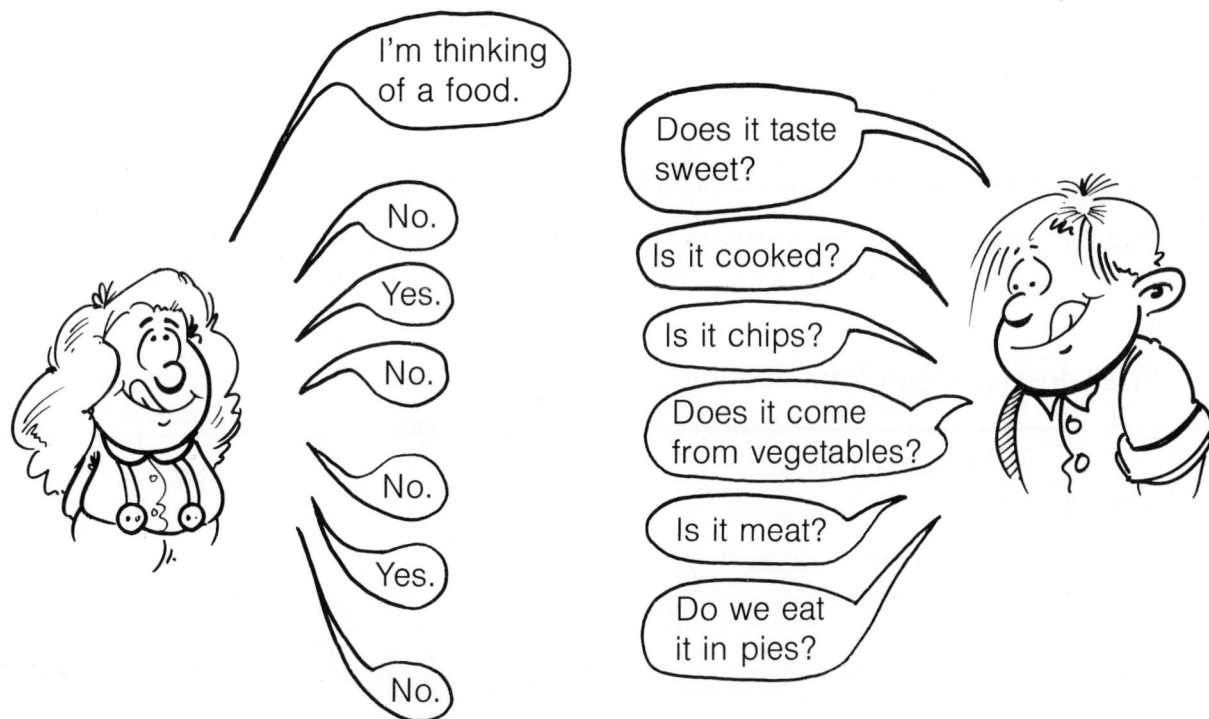

I'm thinking of a food.

No.

Yes.

No.

No.

Yes.

No.

Does it taste sweet?

Is it cooked?

Is it chips?

Does it come from vegetables?

Is it meat?

Do we eat it in pies?

What question would you ask next if you were Ian? Can you guess which food Tracey is thinking of?

Did you notice that some questions that Ian asked were better than others? What kind of questions do you think are the best ones to ask?

You can play this game with your friend. Think carefully about the questions you ask. You might find that a reference book will help you ask really good questions.

© David Wray 1991, *The Project Research Pack*, Stanley Thornes (Publishers) Ltd

A food dossier

A dossier is a collection of information about something. A policeman might have a dossier on a criminal; a car salesman might have a dossier on a car he is selling. We can make dossiers on things by collecting information.

Let's start to make a dossier on our favourite foods. Here is a start for the first page.

SUBJECT: Chips

What are they made from?   How are they cooked?
How are they made?   How are they eaten?
What do they contain?

You might be able to think of some other questions to add to this list.

The next step is to find answers to these questions. Some of these answers you will already know, and some you will need to search for in books.

Your dossier might look like this:

Subject: CHIPS

Made from: ....

Made by: ....

Contain: ....

and so on.

When you have done this the first page of your dossier will be complete.

You can add other pages for other kinds of foods.

© David Wray 1991, *The Project Research Pack*, Stanley Thornes (Publishers) Ltd

Activity 3 Vitamins

Listed below are six different types of foods. Opposite are the names of six different vitamins.

Oranges	Vitamin A
Eggs	Vitamin B_{12}
Carrots	Vitamin B_2
Milk	Vitamin C
Broccoli	Vitamin D
Nuts	Vitamin E

Find out from your books which vitamins each of these foods contains and draw lines in the right places on the diagram. A start has already been made for you.

© David Wray 1991, *The Project Research Pack*, Stanley Thornes (Publishers) Ltd

Ingredients

The things we use to cook particular recipes are called ingredients. Some ingredients are used in many different recipes. Some ingredients are obvious, like potatoes, or bacon. You might wonder what some others are.

Do you know what these ingredients are?

Coriander, paprika, aubergines, anchovies, fennel, mozzarella, shallots.

You will be able to find out by looking in cookery books or encyclopaedias. Remember to use the index to speed things up.

When you know what each ingredient is, see if you can find, for each ingredient, a recipe in which it is used. Have you tasted any of the recipes you find?

You can record your information on this table:

Ingredient	Description	Recipe
Coriander		
Paprika		
Aubergines		
Anchovies		
Fennel		
Mozzarella		
Shallots		

© David Wray 1991, *The Project Research Pack*, Stanley Thornes (Publishers) Ltd

What's in our food?

On many food packets now you will find information about what the food contains. On a packet of bread I bought recently I found this table.

NUTRITIONAL INFORMATION	
	per 100 g
Protein	9.4 g
Carbohydrate	44.7 g
Fat	2.8 g
Dietary fibre	3.2 g

We need to have all four of these in our diet somewhere. Can you find out what we need each of them for? Write down what you find like this:

We need protein in our diet because . . .

Look at some other food packaging and note down the amounts that the food has of these four things. Write down the name of the food you find which:

1 Has the most protein
2 Has the most fat
3 Has the most carbohydrate
4 Has the most dietary fibre.

© David Wray 1991, *The Project Research Pack*, Stanley Thornes (Publishers) Ltd

Eating round the world

A friend of mine is going to India soon. He says he is most looking forward to tasting the food there. He gave me a list of the types of food he specially wants to try.

> Lamb Tikka
> Naan bread
> Chicken Kashmir

Have you tasted any of these?

Can you find the names of three other kinds of food you would be able to eat if you visited India?

Try to do the same for these countries:

> Mexico
> China
> France
> Italy

To find this information you will need to look in reference books about each country. Look in the index of each book first for 'food'.

© David Wray 1991, *The Project Research Pack*, Stanley Thornes (Publishers) Ltd

Shopping lists

Imagine you are having friends to stay for the weekend and you have to cook all the meals. Plan what you will cook using the table.

	Saturday	Sunday
Breakfast		
Lunch		
Tea		

You will need to look in some cookery books for suitable recipes to use. Don't forget that each meal can have more than one course.

When you have planned all the meals, make a shopping list of all the ingredients you will need to buy.

Can you find out how much your shopping would cost if you actually bought it?

1½ lbs Stewing Steak	¼lb sliced mushrooms
1 medium onion	¼ pint of red wine
1 pint stock	1 pint of milk
herbs	corn flakes
½lb kidney	bread
1lb sausages	oxo
5lb potatoes	12 oz. puff pastry
tin of peas	packet of cakes
cauliflower	packet of tea bags
½lb butter	jar of marmalade

© David Wray 1991, *The Project Research Pack*, Stanley Thornes (Publishers) Ltd

Handling food

Activity 8

We have to take great care when handling fresh food. If we don't the food might make us ill. We can get food-poisoning, salmonella or listeriosis from badly handled food.

To help stop us suffering from these things, we can make a list of Do's and Don'ts for handling fresh food. The list is started here:

When handling fresh food:	
Do	Don't
Wash your hands thoroughly	Leave food standing out of a fridge for a long time

Can you add to this list?

Some of your reference books might help you with this. 'Hygiene' is one word you might look under in the index.

What other words do you think will be useful?

© David Wray 1991, *The Project Research Pack*, Stanley Thornes (Publishers) Ltd

Activity
9

Advertisements

Advertisements are usually made up of statements which are real facts, and statements which are there just to try to persuade you to buy what is being advertised. We need to be able to tell these statements apart.

Look through some magazines and find an advertisement for an item of food. It might be a specially prepared meal, a type of crisp, a sweet or anything you like.

Make two headings in your book: *Facts*, and *Statements to persuade*. Read your advertisement and try to write down some of the things it says under the right heading. The list below might give you a start. It was taken from an advertisement for cheese.

Facts	Statements to persuade
Contains essential calcium Mild taste	A thousand and one uses Creamy, heavenly taste

Imagine you were making an item of food which you wanted to sell. Write down some *facts* about this food. Now write down some things you might say about it which you think would make people want to buy it.

Using a mixture of these facts and statements to persuade, design your own advertisement for your food. Look at some advertisements in magazines to get some ideas for how to set your advertisement out.

Galbani
The name to trust

For decades, the Galbani name has stood for quality and value. Galbani cheeses are highly nutritious, exceptionally tasty and much lower in calories than most people realise.

Galbani cheeses are not only an essential part of a healthy, balanced diet, they are also a vital part of tastier eating.

DOLCELATTE
Galbani
Galbani

© David Wray 1991, *The Project Research Pack*, Stanley Thornes (Publishers) Ltd

The Romans

USING THE ACTIVITIES

The appropriateness of these activities for particular groups of children will depend upon a number of things, including their previous experience with this kind of work. Teachers are therefore urged to use the activity sheets as they think appropriate. A tentative grading might, however, be as follows:

Lower juniors (ages 7–9): Activities 3, 4, 5, 6
Upper juniors (ages 9–11): Activities 1, 2, 7, 8, 9

These activities can be done as self-contained exercises, but they will all benefit greatly from discussion beforehand, and (especially) afterwards. All the sheets will work best if tackled by two or three children together.

In the case of Activities 3, 4, 5, 6 and 7 discussion will be needed beforehand to point out the use of reference sources to the children, and afterwards to draw their attention to the way they were able to use these sources.

SKILLS TO BE DEVELOPED

Activity 1
The children are here asked to pose questions about their topic from a special point of view. They will probably need some discussion beforehand about the job of an archaeologist, and an ideal beginning to this activity, and to the project in general, would be a visit to some local Roman remains.

Activity 2
The idea that not all questions are capable of being answered may be unfamiliar to children, and this activity will require a good deal of discussion. It leads well into later work about facts and opinions.

Activity 3
This is a straightforward information-finding and matching task. It focuses particularly upon the use of an index to locate information.

Activity 4
Another straightforward information-finding task. Children may need some help in deciding which words to look for in index pages.

Activity 5
This activity involves the selection of information. Children will have to combine the use of their reference books with the use of a modern atlas. They may need some guidance in the most efficient ways to use these different information sources.

Activity 6
This activity again requires the location of particular information. The children will be looking for dates and this provides a good opportunity to introduce them to the technique of scanning – that is, glancing quickly at a page to find a specific piece of information. The drawing up of a time-line might be difficult for some of them and may require some preliminary work.

Activity 7
The end product of this activity will be a report based upon real information, which children need to locate. This use of information may be unfamiliar to them and they will probably need some guidance with the writing task.

Activity 8
This is an extended activity which focuses upon the organisation of information. It could be preceded by a visit to some local Roman remains, or a look at some slides on Roman Britain, so that children could get a first hand look at the kind of thing which it would be helpful to produce.

Activity 9
Distinguishing between fact and opinion is an important element in the evaluation of information. It should be pointed out to children that books sometimes contain opinions which are presented as facts.

Skills analysis

Topic: The Romans	Skill stage				
	1	2	3	4	5
Activity 1	√				
Activity 2	√				
Activity 3		√			
Activity 4		√			
Activity 5		√	√		
Activity 6		√	√	√	
Activity 7		√	√	√	
Activity 8		√	√	√	
Activity 9		√	√		√

Activity

1

Be an archaeologist

An archaeologist is someone who finds out things about the way people lived in the past. The archaeologist starts with any evidence there is about the past, such as the remains of buildings, and then asks questions about his evidence.

Imagine you are an archaeologist. You have discovered the ruins of a Roman villa buried beneath a mound of earth.

After examining the ruins there would be lots of questions you would want to ask.

You might want to ask:
How was this villa built?
What were each of the rooms for?
How many people would have lived here?
How did these people live?

Can you think of other questions you might ask about what you have found?

Real archaeologists have done just this with the ruins which have been found of real Roman buildings. Find out about some real Roman ruins.

When you have thought of the questions to ask about them, you might be able to answer some of them by looking in books written about the archaeologists' findings.

Are there any questions which you cannot answer? If there are, you might think whether these questions are impossible to answer, or whether more evidence is needed to answer them.

© David Wray 1991, *The Project Research Pack*, Stanley Thornes (Publishers) Ltd

Possible and impossible questions

We usually think of questions as being things we can answer. But some questions are impossible to answer.

Read the questions in the list below.

1 When did the Romans come to Britain?
2 What did the Britons think about their arrival?
3 How long did the Romans stay in Britain?
4 What would have happened if the Romans had not left Britain?
5 What did the Romans leave behind in Britain?

Which of these questions do you think are possible to answer? Which are impossible?

You may have realised that it is impossible to know what the Britons really thought about the arrival of the Romans. Because the Britons at that time did not use writing, the only written accounts we have are of what the Romans thought the Britons felt. They might have been wrong.

It is also impossible to know what would have happened if the Romans had not left Britain. There are many possible ways things could have gone.

Make two headings in your book.

Questions we can answer	Impossible questions

Write some questions of your own about the Romans under each of these headings.

© David Wray 1991, *The Project Research Pack*, Stanley Thornes (Publishers) Ltd

Roman gods

The Romans had many gods. They told many stories about the adventures of the gods which you will enjoy reading.

In the list below are the names of some of their gods. Opposite each name you are told what that god was the god of. Unfortunately these two lists have been mixed up. Mars was not the god of the sea but of war, for example.

Can you sort out the list by drawing lines from each god to what he (or she) was really god (or goddess) of? One has already been done for you.

Mars	The sea
Jupiter	Hunting
Minerva	War
Neptune	King of the gods
Pluto	Music and poetry
Venus	Wisdom
Diana	The underworld
Apollo	Love

Remember to use the index of the books you use to help you.

© David Wray 1991, *The Project Research Pack*, Stanley Thornes (Publishers) Ltd

Activity 4

True or false?

Here are ten sentences about the Romans. Some of them are true and some are false. Can you say which is which? You will have to use reference books to find out. Remember to use the contents and the index pages.

1 The founders of Rome, Romulus and Remus, were brought up by a wolf.

2 The first Roman emperor was called Augustus.

3 Julius Caesar conquered Britain with his armies.

4 Egypt was part of the Roman empire.

5 The emperor Nero is said to have played a harp while Rome was burning.

6 Hadrian's wall was built to protect Roman Britain from the fierce Welsh tribes.

7 The first Roman emperor to visit Britain was Claudius.

8 Rome was conquered by Hannibal of Carthage and his army of elephants.

9 The Roman army was organised into legions, each under the command of a centurion.

10 Gladiators used to fight each other, sometimes to the death, to amuse the Roman crowds.

Make up some sentences like this for yourself. See if your friend can tell which are true and which false.

© David Wray 1991, *The Project Research Pack*, Stanley Thornes (Publishers) Ltd

Activity
5

The Roman empire

Here is a map of the world of the Romans.

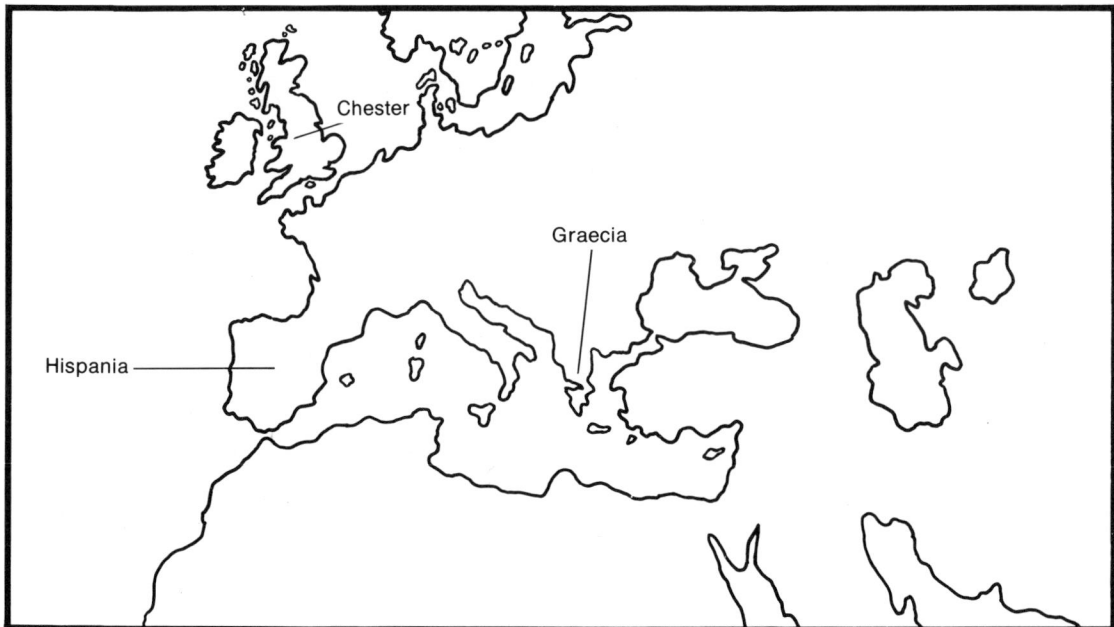

Chester

Graecia

Hispania

On this map try to mark some of the places which were part of the Roman Empire. Some have already been marked for you, but can you find out where these places were and mark them on the map?

Gaul

Londinium

Palestine

Alexandria

Damascus

Carthage

You will find some of these places in modern atlases, but for some you might need to look in your reference books first.

Colour in the countries on the map which were at one time part of the Roman Empire.

© David Wray 1991, *The Project Research Pack*, Stanley Thornes (Publishers) Ltd

Activity 6

The Roman emperors

Here are the names of six Roman emperors:

Vespasian
Hadrian
Augustus
Claudius
Tiberius
Nero

Do you know which of these was the first Roman emperor?

Can you arrange the rest in the correct order?

Remember to look in the index of the books you use for this.

On the time-line which is drawn alongside this page write the names of these emperors in their correct places.

Can you add the names of any other emperors to the time line?

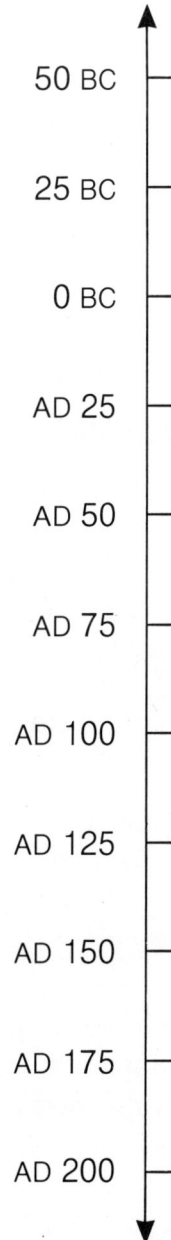

50 BC

25 BC

0 BC

AD 25

AD 50

AD 75

AD 100

AD 125

AD 150

AD 175

AD 200

© David Wray 1991, *The Project Research Pack*, Stanley Thornes (Publishers) Ltd

Roman Britain

Activity 7

The Romans invaded and conquered Britain. There are many remains still visible which tell us about this period of history.

See if you can find out some things about the Romans in Britain from your books.

Try to find the answers to these questions. Just jot down your answers as quick notes for the moment.

1 When did the Romans first come to Britain?

2 Why did they come?

3 When did they begin to settle in Britain?

4 Who were their leaders?

5 Where in Britain did they build towns?

6 How did they improve the transport system?

7 How much of Britain did they conquer?

8 What did they do about the parts they did not conquer?

9 What did the people who already lived in Britain do?

When you have got all this information, try to use it to write the story of:

The Roman conquest of Britain.

If you include some pictures of Roman soldiers, British warriors and some maps and diagrams, your story will make a useful booklet to display with the rest of your Roman project work.

© David Wray 1991, *The Project Research Pack*, Stanley Thornes (Publishers) Ltd

Activity 8

A Roman trail

There are many places in Britain with Roman remains. There are forts, houses, bridges, roads, theatres and baths. On the map of Britain mark some of the most important remains.

For each of the places you mark see if you can find out:

What was this place like in Roman times?

What can be seen there now?

Using this information you can write a short guidebook for anyone who wants to visit the important Roman remains in Britain. This guide to the 'Roman Trail' should tell readers:

Where to go

What they will see there

What this tells us about the Romans in Britain.

© David Wray 1991, The Project Research Pack, Stanley Thornes (Publishers) Ltd

Facts and opinions

Read the following sentences about the Romans.

The Romans came from Rome in Italy.

They were a very well organised and clever people.

They built up a very large empire.

They lost this empire because they became lazy.

Two of these sentences give *facts* about the Romans, and two of them give people's *opinions*. Can you decide which is which?

Facts are things that we know are true, because we can prove them. Opinions are things people believe to be true, but which cannot really be proved. Do you think your reference books are more likely to have facts or opinions in them?

Look in a reference book about the Romans and find three sentences which you think give facts, and three which you think give opinions. Discuss your sentences with your friends. Do you all agree which are facts and which opinions?

© David Wray 1991, *The Project Research Pack*, Stanley Thornes (Publishers) Ltd

Animals

USING THE ACTIVITIES

The appropriateness of these activities for particular groups of children will depend upon a number of things, including their previous experience with this kind of work. Teachers are therefore urged to use the activity sheets as they think appropriate. A tentative grading might, however, be as follows:

Lower juniors (ages 7–9): Activities 1, 3, 4, 5, 6
Upper juniors (ages 9–11): Activities 2, 7, 8, 9

These activities can be done as self-contained exercises, but they will all benefit greatly from discussion beforehand, and (especially) afterwards. All the activities will work best if tackled by two or three children together.

In the case of Activities 3, 4, 5, 6 and 7 discussion will be needed beforehand to point out the use of reference sources to the children, and afterwards to draw their attention to they way they were able to use these sources. For sheet 8 the sources required will be wider than the normal reference books and will include pamphlets and magazines.

SKILLS TO BE DEVELOPED

Activity 1
The activity is intended to get children to ask questions as a preliminary to answering them. They should be encouraged to do this prior to most information handling tasks. The activity also encourages some discussion about the best ways of finding information.

Activity 2
This introduces the idea of a collection of information. It focuses upon the formulation of questions, but will give an opportunity for practice of location skills as children try to answer their questions. A useful extension would be to introduce the children to data-handling programs on the computer. Their dossiers will give a framework for the construction of a computer database.

Activity 3
This activity requires the location of particular information. The children will be looking for figures (heights or weights, whichever they decide) and this provides a good opportunity to introduce them to the technique of scanning – that is, glancing quickly at a page to find a specific piece of information. They will also be getting experience in using an index, which again demands some scanning ability.

Activity 4
This extends the skills developed in the previous activity. The children have to find specific pieces of information about particular animals. They are introduced to a list-type presentation of information. The activity could also be used to tie in with mathematical sorting activities.

Activity 5
This activity has a dual purpose. Its main purpose is to get children to select particular pieces of information from a larger collection. It also asks them to make judgements on the basis of the information they find, and to discuss their judgements with other children.

Activity 6
This is a simple activity which asks children to consider carefully the information they can provide about an animal without giving its name away. They have not only to select information but to think about it from the point of view of someone else.

Activity 7
The children are introduced here to a particular way of organising information using a grid format. They also, of course, have to be able to find the information they require. Children often find the grid format difficult and completed grids can be used as a focus for discussion with other children.

Activity 8
The children are introduced here to a different way of organising information, and they are asked both to use the tree structure and to extend it. They may be familiar with this kind of format from work on the computer. 'Animals' is used in a broad sense to include mammals, birds, reptiles and fish.

Activity 9
Distinguishing between fact and opinion is an important element in the evaluation of information. It should be pointed out to children that books sometimes contain opinions which are presented as facts.

Skills analysis

Topic: Animals	Skill stage				
	1	2	3	4	5
Activity 1	√				
Activity 2	√				
Activity 3		√	√		
Activity 4		√	√		
Activity 5		√	√		
Activity 6		√	√		
Activity 7		√	√	√	
Activity 8				√	
Activity 9				√	√

Ask about...

Look at this picture of an animal.

Asela liked this picture. There were lots of questions he wanted to ask about it.

1 What kind of animal is it?
2 Where does it come from?
3 What does it eat?
4 Is it dangerous to humans?

What other questions could Asela ask?

Find your own picture of an animal. Show it to your friend and get your friend to ask you questions about it. Can you answer your friend's questions? If there are any you cannot answer, do you know how to find the answers?

© David Wray 1991, *The Project Research Pack*, Stanley Thornes (Publishers) Ltd

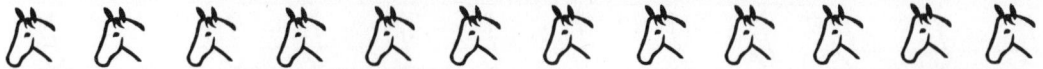

An animal dossier

A dossier is a collection of information about something. An accountant might have a dossier on a company; a doctor might have a dossier on a patient. We can make dossiers on things by collecting information.

Let's start to make a dossier on some animals we know about. Here is a start for the first page.

ANIMAL: Elephant

Where does it come from?
What types are there?
What kind of countryside does it live in?
What does it eat?
How can you tell males from females?

You might be able to think of some other questions to add to this list.

The next step is to find answers to these questions. Some of these answers you will already know, and some you will need to search for in books.

Your dossier might look like this:

Subject: ELEPHANTS

Come from: . . . .

Types: . . . .

Habitat: . . . .

and so on. . .

When you have done this the first page of your dossier will be complete.

You can add other pages for other animals.

© David Wray 1991, *The Project Research Pack*, Stanley Thornes (Publishers) Ltd

Biggest and smallest

Here are pictures of some animals.

A Blue Whale

Height . . . . . .
Weight . . . . . .

A Shrew

Height . . . . . .
Weight . . . . . .

A Giraffe

Height . . . . . .
Weight . . . . . .

An Elephant

Height . . . . . .
Weight . . . . . .

A Wombat

Height . . . . . .
Weight . . . . . .

A Hippopotamus

Height . . . . . .
Weight . . . . . .

Can you find out the average heights and weights of these animals and write this information in each box? You will need to use your reference books carefully for this. Then cut out each box and arrange the animals in order of size, putting the smallest first and the biggest last.

Can you find an animal that is bigger than the biggest in your list, and one that is smaller than the smallest in your list?

Remember to check this carefully in your books.

© David Wray 1991, *The Project Research Pack*, Stanley Thornes (Publishers) Ltd

Activity 4

Sorting animals

Here is a list of some animals you may have heard about.

Can you add the names of three or four other animals to the list?

Gnu, Porpoise, Emu, Conger, Dingo, Albatross, Wallaby, Turbot, Terrapin, Guillemot, Piranha, Iguana . . . .

Sort out your list of animals in the following three ways.

Remember you will need to use reference books to help you.

1 Where do these animals spend most of their time?

   Write the name of each animal under the right heading in your book.

On land	In the water	In the air

2 What kind of animals are they?

   Write the name of each animal under the right heading in your book.

Mammal	Bird	Reptile	Fish

3 In which countries are they found?

Write the name of each animal in your book and then write the country (or countries) in which it can be found beside each animal.

Can you think of any other ways of sorting out these animals?

© David Wray 1991, *The Project Research Pack*, Stanley Thornes (Publishers) Ltd

Activity
5

Which is best?

Look at this list of animals. All of them help us in some way.

Horse   Cow

Elephant   Goat

Cat   Sheep

Use your reference books to find out the ways in which each of these animals helps us.

Can you decide which of these animals is the most important to us?

Using the information you have found, write a paragraph explaining your reasons for choosing this animal.

Show what you have written to somebody else who has done this sheet. Do you both agree on your choice of animal? If not, try to persuade your friend that your choice is the best.

© David Wray 1991, *The Project Research Pack*, Stanley Thornes (Publishers) Ltd

Activity

6

Animal clues

I am thinking of an animal.
Can you guess its name?
Here are some clues to help
you.

1 This animal lives in India.
2 It is very fierce.
3 Its coat is striped.
4 It is a kind of cat.

Have you guessed it?

Here is a picture of it.

Play this game with your friends. You have to think of an animal and
give them some clues about it. They have to try to guess its name.

You will need to look in reference books to help you choose which clues
to give.

© David Wray 1991, *The Project Research Pack*, Stanley Thornes (Publishers) Ltd

Animal facts

Down the left hand side of the grid below write the names of ten animals you have heard about.

For each of these animals try to answer the questions along the top of the grid. Put the answers in the correct boxes.

Remember that you will need to use the contents and index pages of the reference books you look in.

Questions / Names of animals	What colour is it?	Where does it live?	What does it eat?	Do any animals eat it?
1				
2				
3				
4				
5				
6				
7				
8				
9				
10				

© David Wray 1991, *The Project Research Pack*, Stanley Thornes (Publishers) Ltd

Animal trees

One way of sorting out information is to use a tree diagram. Here is an example of one to do with kinds of animals.

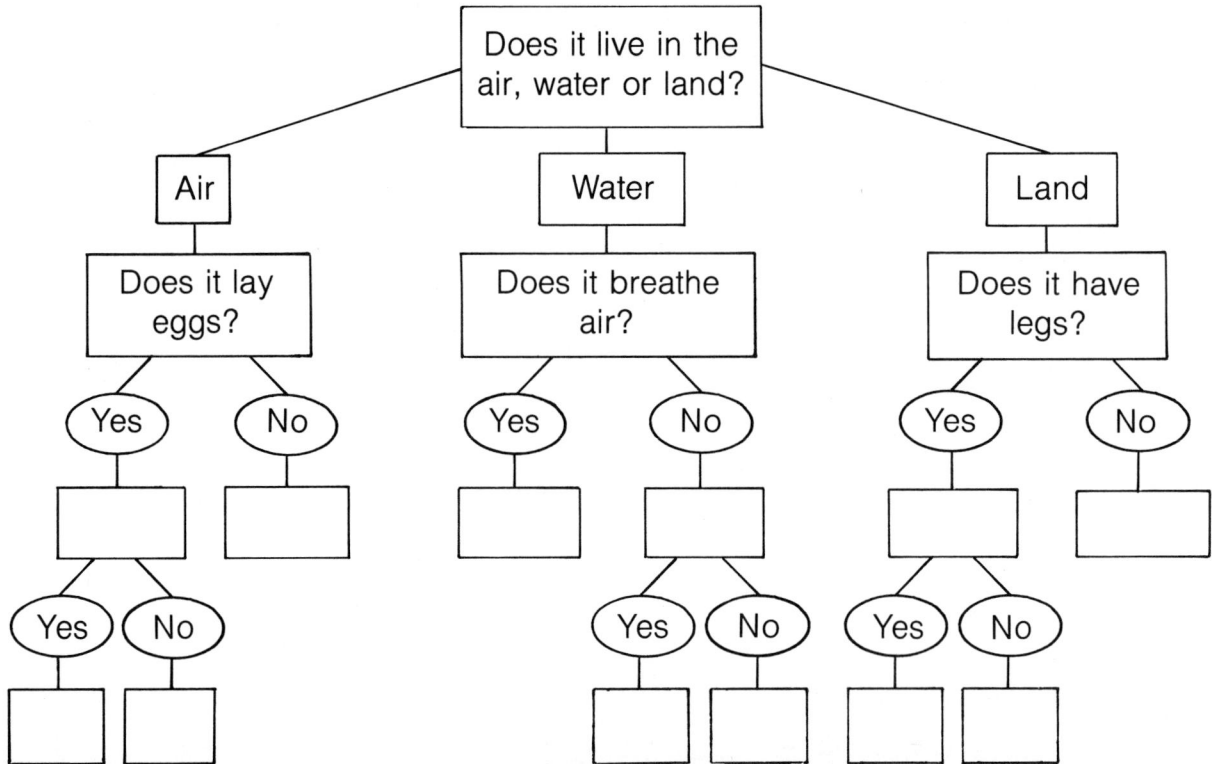

Does it live in the air, water or land?

Air
Water
Land

Does it lay eggs?
Does it breathe air?
Does it have legs?

Yes   No
Yes   No
Yes   No

Yes   No
Yes   No
Yes   No

Where an empty box is followed by 'Yes' or 'No' fill it in with the right question. Where a branch of the tree ends, fill in the empty box with the name of an animal.

You will need to follow the questions through and find out the information you need from your books.

Can you add any more questions to the bottom of the branches of the tree?

© David Wray 1991, *The Project Research Pack*, Stanley Thornes (Publishers) Ltd

Activity
9

Looking after our wildlife

Many people are worried about the wildlife of the world, especially some of the animals. Some people say that animals such as tigers, elephants and whales may be extinct in a few years. What do you think about this?

Try to find some information about this topic. You will need to look in reference books, pamphlets, magazines and newspapers.

As you read the information you find, try to make some notes in your book using these two headings. You will need to discuss where each note should go with your partner.

Facts	Opinions

Use the information you have collected to write your own pamphlet with the title:

The Future of Our Animals.

Amanda Wood / World Wildlife Fund

© David Wray 1991, *The Project Research Pack*, Stanley Thornes (Publishers) Ltd

Our town

USING THE ACTIVITIES

The appropriateness of these activities for particular groups of children will depend upon a number of things, including their previous experience with this kind of work. Teachers are therefore urged to use the activity sheets as they think appropriate. A tentative grading might, however, be as follows:

Lower juniors (ages 7–9): Activities 1, 3, 4, 6
Upper juniors (ages 9–11): Activities 2, 5, 7, 8, 9

These activities can be done as self-contained exercises, but they will all benefit greatly from discussion beforehand, and (especially) afterwards. All the activities will work best if tackled by two or three children together.

In the case of activities 3, 4, 6 and 7 discussion will be needed beforehand to point out the use of reference sources to the children, and afterwards to draw their attention to the way they were able to use these sources. The sources required will be wider than the normal reference books and will include *The Yellow Pages*, local guidebooks, tourist material etc. Try to have a supply of this material to hand, but do not give it to the children straight away. They will gain a lot from discussing what sources they need and trying to obtain these themselves.

SKILLS TO BE DEVELOPED

Activity 1
This activity is intended to start children thinking about the subject of the project. It focuses particularly upon the asking of questions, a stage all project work should begin with. This activity could be the preliminary to a much larger activity as children attempt to design and write their town guide.

Activity 2
This activity also focuses upon the asking of questions. It asks them to put themselves into another person's shoes, which may prove difficult for some of them. In this case a useful way in is to ask them to imagine they are visitors to a new town and to list the things they would want to know.

Activity 3
This is a fairly straightforward information-finding task. The fact-file activity can be used in most projects. Here it may be slightly more difficult because the information needed will not be found in traditional reference books. Encourage the children

to discuss and find possible sources of this information for themselves. You might, of course, also have some sources to hand, to be used only if the children are really stuck.

Activity 4
Another information-finding task. It would be useful to have a few copies of the local Yellow Pages handy, although the children might think of and find alternative sources for this information.

Activity 5
This activity involves the children in choosing particular pieces of information to fit the needs of particular people. They may need help in seeing things from other peoples' points of view. The activity will help develop their abilities to read in special ways, such as skimming for a general impression and scanning for particular information.

Activity 6
In this activity they will again be asked to scan sources of information for particular facts. The information they require will probably be in the form of figures so this is a reasonably easy introduction to scanning.

Activity 7
Here children are asked to find several pieces of information and then to reorganise them into the form of a newspaper report. Many of them will need to be given some experience of reading newspaper reports and discussing their content and style. This could profitably be done as a series of whole class lessons. In writing their reports children might be able to use a newspaper emulation computer programme such as *Front Page Extra*.

Activity 8
This is an extended activity which focuses upon the organisation of information. It would benefit greatly from being preceded by a tour of the town, so that children could get a first hand look at the kind of thing which it would be helpful to produce.

Activity 9
This activity introduces children to the evaluation of information by asking them to produce 'persuasive' information deliberately. Doing this should raise their awareness of how information can be presented in this way, and, hopefully, make them more circumspect about it in everyday life.

Skills analysis

Topic: Our town	Skill stage				
	1	2	3	4	5
Activity 1	√				
Activity 2	√				
Activity 3		√			
Activity 4		√			
Activity 5		√	√		
Activity 6		√	√		
Activity 7		√	√	√	
Activity 8				√	
Activity 9					√

Activity 1

A town guide

Is there a guide book for your town?

It would be interesting to try to write one.

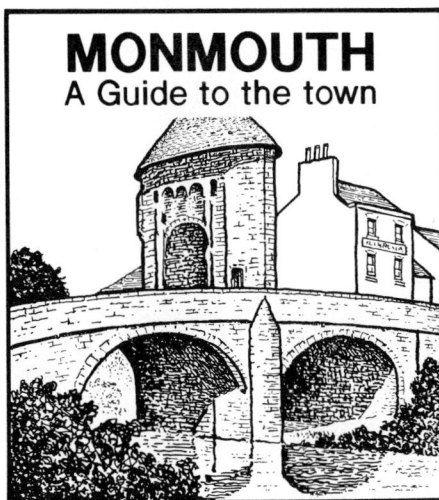

MONMOUTH
A Guide to the town

The first thing a writer of any guide book must decide is what will be included in the guide.

Will it include things like:

The history of the town?
Famous events which have taken place in the town?
A list of the shops in the town?
A town plan?

Make a list of the things you would want to include in a guide book for your town. Show your list to some of your friends and see if they can add things to it.

Can you arrange your list into topics?

Each topic could be the start of a chapter in the guide book.

During your 'Town Project' you might get the chance to write a town guide book. Your list of topics will help you do this.

© David Wray 1991, *The Project Research Pack*, Stanley Thornes (Publishers) Ltd

A visitor to town

Activity 2

What would a visitor to your town want to see?

What might the visitor want to know about these things?

What questions might the visitor ask about your town?

Write two headings in your book.

Things to see	Questions to ask

Under the heading *Things to see* write down the names of some things you think a visitor to your town might want to see. For each of these things write down under the heading *Questions to ask* some questions which the visitor might ask about it.

Can you think of any other questions a visitor might ask about your town?

© David Wray 1991, *The Project Research Pack*, Stanley Thornes (Publishers) Ltd

A town fact-file

Here is a fact-file sheet which has not been filled in yet.

A FACT-FILE ON . . . .

Name of town: . . . .

Population: . . . .

County: . . . .

Telephone dialling code: . . . .

Post code: . . . .

Railway station address: . . . .

Bus station address: . . . .

Names of big hotels: . . . .

. . . .

Can you fill in the fact-file for your town?

There is plenty of space on the fact-file sheet so that you can fill in some extra information of your own.

You will need to think carefully about where you will get the information from.

© David Wray 1991, *The Project Research Pack*, Stanley Thornes (Publishers) Ltd

Activity 4

Shopping

Suppose I wanted to come to your town to buy a new washing machine. Could you tell me the names of the shops I could go to?

You might be able to find a local directory which will give this kind of information.

See if you can find the names and addresses of the nearest one of each of these shops to where you live. Write them on the chart.

	Name	Address
Florist's shop		
Butcher's shop		
Furniture shop		
Electrical shop		
Book shop		
Supermarket		
Clothes shop		
Jewellery shop		

If you can find a plan of your town you could mark the position of these shops on it.

© David Wray 1991, *The Project Research Pack*, Stanley Thornes (Publishers) Ltd

What information do you need?

As part of your project on 'Our town' you have probably collected a lot of information about your town. Some pieces of information are more useful than others to certain people.

Think about the information which the people below might need about your town. For each of these people write down the information which you think would be most valuable.

	Useful information
A tourist	
A businessman wanting to build a factory	
A person interested in history	
A visitor on a shopping trip	
A family with children about to start school	

© David Wray 1991, *The Project Research Pack*, Stanley Thornes (Publishers) Ltd

Activity 6

Populations

Look at the list of towns below. If your town is not there already then add it to the list. Against each town write down the number of people living in it – its population. You will need to think carefully about where you will get this information from.

Town	Population
Brighton	
Peterborough	
Leeds	
York	
Aberdeen	
Cardiff	
Exeter	
Newcastle	
Edinburgh	
Carlisle	
Manchester	
Shrewsbury	
Oxford	

Which of these towns has the most people living in it?

Write down the name of the town in your book. Underneath it write down the town with the second largest population, and then the third, and so on.

Can you find a town in Britain with a larger population than any of these?

© David Wray 1991, *The Project Research Pack*, Stanley Thornes (Publishers) Ltd

An important event in our town

Has anything important ever happened in your town? You may have had an important historical event, or perhaps something happened once which your town celebrates still.

If you can think of an important event here are some questions about it which you can try to answer. You might find answers in reference books, in local town history books, or in the local museum.

1 When did this event happen?

2 Whereabouts did it take place?

3 Who was involved in it?

4 What actually happened?

5 What was the result?

6 How is the event remembered nowadays?

When you have found out as much as you can, imagine you were writing a report about this event for the local newspaper. Write your report in the way that a newspaper reporter would. Remember you will need an exciting headline and, perhaps, a photograph as well.

© David Wray 1991, *The Project Research Pack*, Stanley Thornes (Publishers) Ltd

A town trail

You will probably have been on a nature trail. These often go through woods or other interesting parts of the countryside. They have places where you stop to look around you, and a booklet tells you which interesting things you should look at.

A town trail would be the same, but in a town.

Can you design a town trail for your town? These are some of the things you will need to do.

Make a list of some interesting places in your town.

Mark these places on a map of your town.

Work out a route around the town, visiting some of these places. You will need to think about how long your trail will take to walk around. If it is too long, it might be better to prepare two separate trails.

Write some information notes for people to read when they reach each place on the trail.

Design and make a trail booklet. This should contain:
A map to guide people around the trail
Information for them to read when they come to the interesting places
A list of places they might go if they want to find out more about your town.

When you have completed your town trail you might show it to your local library or museum. They might want to buy it!

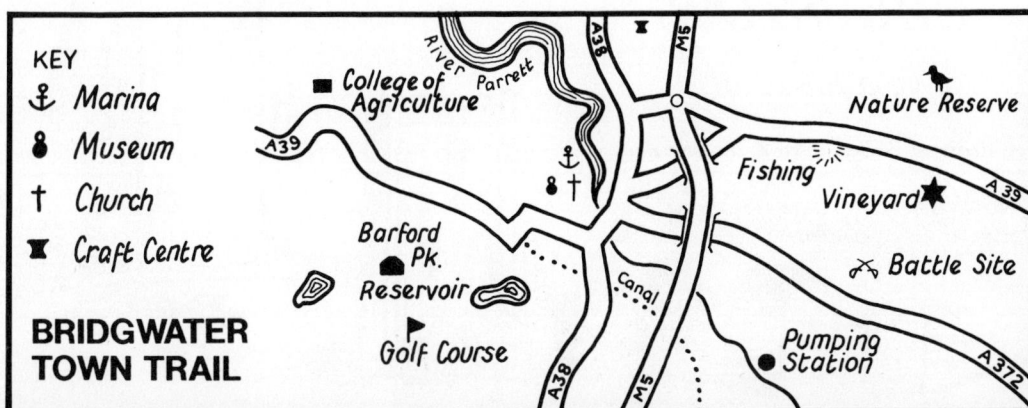

KEY
⚓ Marina
⚱ Museum
† Church
⚒ Craft Centre

BRIDGWATER
TOWN TRAIL

College of Agriculture
River Parrett
Nature Reserve
Fishing
Vineyard
Barford Pk.
Reservoir
Battle Site
Canal
Golf Course
Pumping Station

© David Wray 1991, *The Project Research Pack*, Stanley Thornes (Publishers) Ltd

An advert for your town

Does your town get lots of visitors? Whether it does or not, one way of increasing the number of visitors is to advertise the town.

How would you advertise your town to persuade people to come and visit it?

To help you think about this it would be useful to collect some examples of advertisements for other towns which you might find in magazines, newspapers or brochures. How do these advertisements go about trying to persuade people to visit places?

You will also need to think about what your town has which might attract visitors. This might include historical buildings, nice surrounding countryside, lovely parks, good shops, interesting museums and so on.

Now try to design some advertisements for your town. These might be the kind of advertisements you would see in magazines, or you might be able to make a short video advertisement, or a radio advertisement using a tape-recorder.

After making your advertisements you need to try them out on your friends. Ask your friends if the advertisements made them want to visit your town, and why. This might give you some clues about how you might redesign your advertisement.

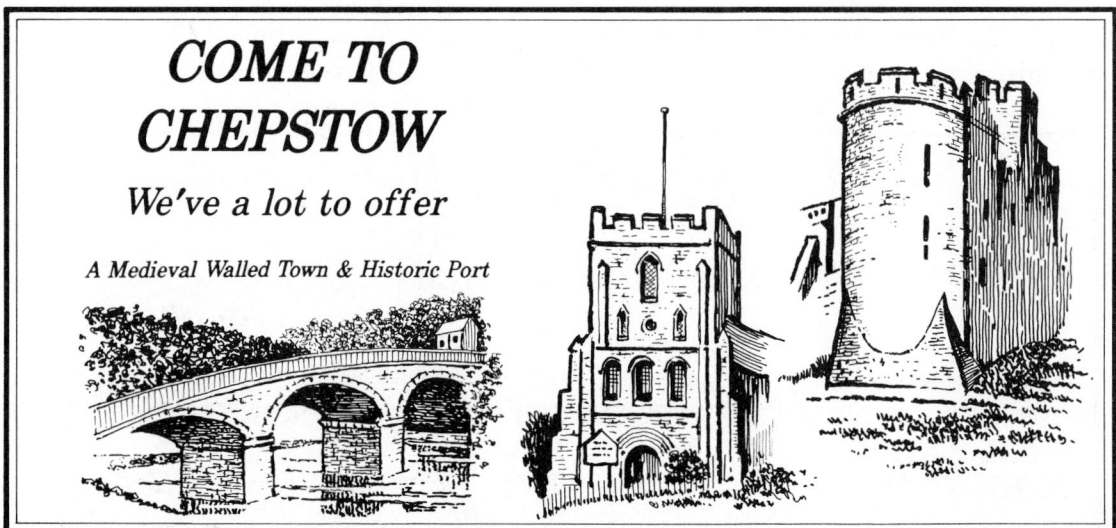

> ## COME TO CHEPSTOW
> *We've a lot to offer*
>
> *A Medieval Walled Town & Historic Port*

© David Wray 1991, *The Project Research Pack*, Stanley Thornes (Publishers) Ltd

Holidays

USING THE ACTIVITIES

The appropriateness of these activities for particular groups of children will depend upon a number of things, including their previous experience with this kind of work. Teachers are therefore urged to use the activity sheets as they think appropriate. A tentative grading might, however, be as follows:

Lower juniors (ages 7–9): Activities 2, 3, 5, 8
Upper juniors (ages 9–11): Activities 1, 4, 6, 7, 9

These activities can be done as self-contained exercises, but they will all benefit greatly from discussion beforehand, and (especially) afterwards.

In the case of Activities 3 and 4 discussion will be needed beforehand to point out the use of atlases as sources of information. Activities 6, 8 and 9 will benefit from some discussion beforehand of the purpose and nature of holiday brochures.

SKILLS TO BE DEVELOPED

Activity 1
This activity focuses upon the asking of questions. It asks children to put themselves into another person's shoes, although they should be able to do the activity from their own experience of taking holidays. This might be a useful activity for them to take home so as to involve their family.

Activity 2
This asks children to think about what they are looking for before consulting information sources. This is a very important habit for them to get into. The activity specifically invites family involvement and is a direct preparation for Activity 6 in which they are asked to use their list of preferences to choose a suitable holiday resort.

Activity 3
This is a fairly straightforward information-finding activity which demands the use of an atlas. Children will need to be shown how to use the index in an atlas to locate particular places.

Activity 4
Another information-finding activity. Children may be able to use only the atlas, if they know about using its index. They may also use a gazeteer and/or series of travel books.

Activity 5
The children are asked in this activity to locate particular information about places of their choice and then to arrange it in a particular way. As a result of this activity they should have the beginning of their own information resource which they will need to arrange sensibly so that they and others can use it subsequently.

Activity 6
The children are introduced here to a particular way of organising information using a grid format. They also, of course, have to be able to find the information they require. They will use holiday brochures as their main source of information for this, but they will need alerting to the possibility that their information may not be entirely accurate. Activity 9 would be a good accompaniment to this.

Activity 7
Here the children are asked to find particular information and then to set it out in a particular way. The information will probably require a fair amount of interpretation before it is entered on the two lists.

Activity 8
The end product of this activity will be a piece of imaginative writing, but it will be based upon real information, which children need to locate. This use of information may be unfamiliar to them and they will probably need some guidance with the writing task.

Activity 9
This activity aims to get children to look critically at and evaluate the information they find, in this case in holiday brochures. The activity of designing their own brochure can be very beneficial in alerting them to the way persuasive techniques work.

95

Skills analysis

Topic: Holidays	Skill stage				
	1	2	3	4	5
Activity 1	√				
Activity 2	√				
Activity 3		√			
Activity 4		√			
Activity 5			√		
Activity 6		√	√		
Activity 7		√	√	√	
Activity 8		√	√	√	
Activity 9					√

Activity 1

The good holiday guide

I am a spy from the *Good Holiday Guide*. I visit lots of holiday resorts to check that they really offer what they say they do in their brochures.

I carry with me a checklist of things to find out about the resort.

My checklist begins like this:

CHECKLIST

1 Is the resort easy to get to?
2 Are the people in the resort friendly?

. . . .

. . . .

. . . .

. . . .

. . . .

What other questions do you think I should include on my checklist?

Design your own checklist for holiday resorts.
You might find that you can use this checklist when you do go on holiday.

© David Wray 1991, *The Project Research Pack*, Stanley Thornes (Publishers) Ltd

Activity
2

What do you want from a holiday?

You probably know the kind of holiday you would really like to take if you could.

I have begun to make a list of the things I would like when I go on holiday. My list begins:

> Lots of sunshine
>
> Exciting activities
>
> Good food.

Make your own list of things you would like to find on holiday.

Ask your family and friends to make their own lists too.

Do all the lists mention the same things?

If you were all going on holiday together, could you find a place to go which would please everybody?

© David Wray 1991, *The Project Research Pack*, Stanley Thornes (Publishers) Ltd

Activity 3: Where have you been on holiday?

Look at this map of Europe.

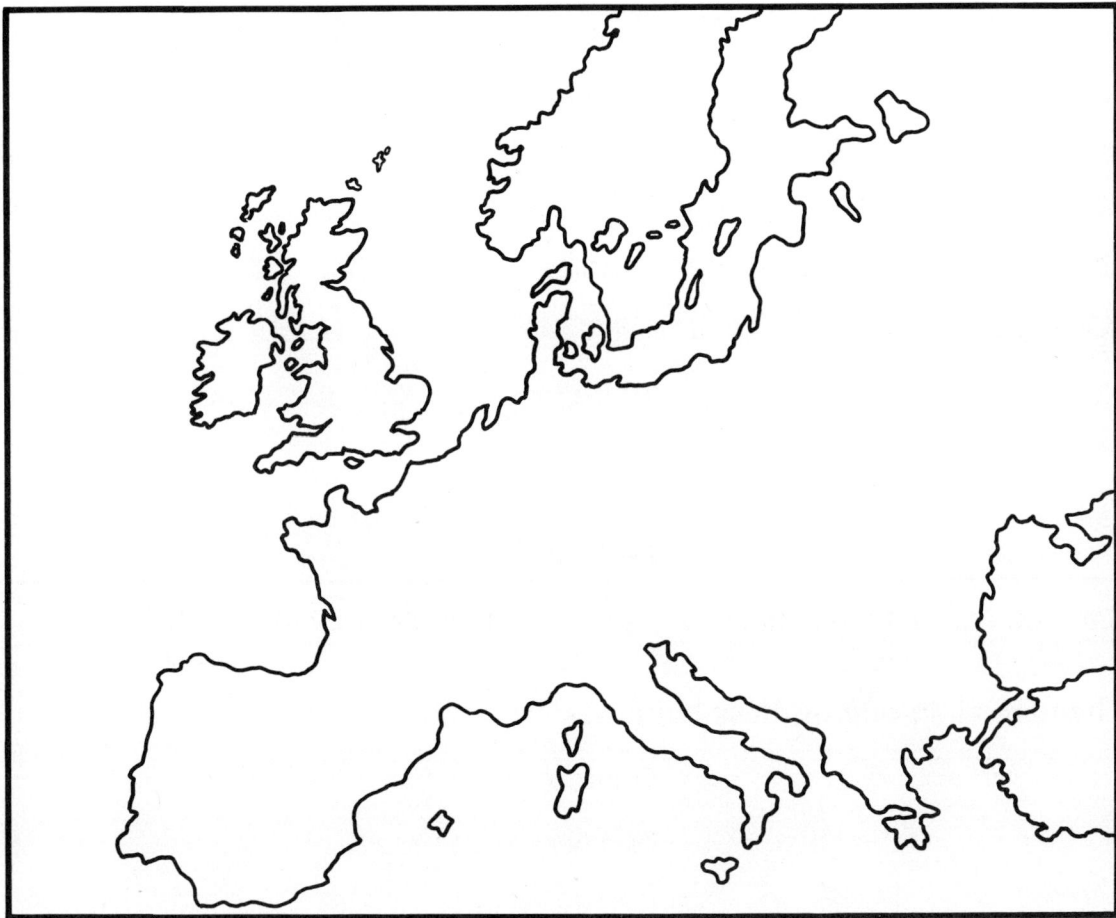

Can you mark on this map the places you have been on holiday?

Ask some other people in your class to tell you the places they have been for holidays.

Mark all these places on the map as well.

Which is the most popular place?

© David Wray 1991, *The Project Research Pack*, Stanley Thornes (Publishers) Ltd

Which country?

Here is a list of some holiday resorts. You or your friends may have been to some of these on holiday.

Majorca

Verbier

Benidorm

Blackpool

Venice

Rhodes

Biarritz

Mayrhofen

Yarmouth

Albufeira

Crete

Zermatt

Can you sort out these holiday resorts into their countries?

They are all in one of these countries:

Greece

Spain

France

Britain

Italy

Switzerland

Austria

Portugal

Can you find the name of another holiday resort in each of these countries?

© David Wray 1991, *The Project Research Pack*, Stanley Thornes (Publishers) Ltd

A holiday directory

Your friends will have been to several different places for their holidays. Compile a directory of the places they have been.

Each page of the directory should look like this:

Place visited . . . . Date visited . . . .

Things to do . . . .

. . . .

Good points . . . .

. . . .

. . . .

Bad points . . . .

. . . .

. . . .

Photograph or drawing:

You will need to write an index for the directory so that people using it can find the place they want easily.

© David Wray 1991, *The Project Research Pack*, Stanley Thornes (Publishers) Ltd

Choosing a holiday

It is sometimes difficult to choose where to go on holiday. It can help if we decide first what we want from a holiday. A table like this can be useful. I have started to fill it in.

What we want \ Places	Majorca	Blackpool	Lake district
Sunshine	✓		
Swimming	✓	✓	✓
Amusement arcades	✓	✓	

Copy the table into your book, but put your own headings on it. You will need to leave room for about ten holiday places.

Down the side write the things you want when you go on holiday.

Now you need to decide which boxes to put ticks into. On the table I started I knew Majorca was sunny so I put a tick in that box.

Use reference books and holiday brochures to fill in your table.

When you have done this you should find that the place which has the most ticks is probably the best place for you to go on holiday.

© David Wray 1991, *The Project Research Pack*, Stanley Thornes (Publishers) Ltd

Having a good time on holiday

We all want to have a good time on holiday. To help us do this there are some things we need to take care about. Sometimes things can spoil our holidays which we could have prevented.

To help do this, we can make a list of Do's and Don'ts for holidays. The list is started here:

When on holiday:	
Do	Don't
Make a list beforehand of things to take with you.	Lie out in the sun so long that you burn.

Can you add to this list? Some of your reference books might help you with this, and you will also find useful information in holiday brochures.

The holiday of a lifetime

If you were given lots of money to spend on any holiday you wanted to take, where would you go?

Plan your holiday of a lifetime. Use these questions to help you:

Where will you go for your holiday?

Where will you stay?

How will you get there?

How long will you go for?

What will you do when you are there?

What will you visit when you are there?

What souvenirs will you buy?

You need to make sure that all these things are actually possible. Use your reference books and holiday brochures to help you.

When you have made your plans, imagine you have been on this holiday. Write an account of the holiday for your friends to read. You can give it the title:

The Holiday of a Lifetime

© David Wray 1991, *The Project Research Pack*, Stanley Thornes (Publishers) Ltd

Holiday brochures

You have probably used lots of holiday brochures during your holiday project. Always remember that holiday brochures are advertisements. They are written to try to persuade you to take your holiday in that place.

Design your own holiday brochure for a place you have been on holiday.

Look at lots of holiday brochures to see how they are designed. You will probably find you need to think about these things:

Brochures concentrate on the good things in a holiday resort. If there are things which are not so good, the brochure will probably not mention them.

Brochures include attractive photographs taken on sunny days. It never rains in holiday brochures!

Brochures use attractive words to describe the resorts. The sea will be 'sparkling' and the hotels 'luxurious'.

You will need to do these things in your brochure.

Space

USING THE ACTIVITIES

The appropriateness of these activities for particular groups of children will depend upon a number of things, including their previous experience with this kind of work. Teachers are therefore urged to use the activity sheets as they think appropriate. A tentative grading might, however, be as follows:

Lower juniors (ages 7–9): Activities 1, 3, 4, 6, 8
Upper juniors (ages 9–11): Activities 2, 5, 7, 9

These activities can be done as self-contained exercises, but they will all benefit greatly from discussion beforehand, and (especially) afterwards. All the sheets will work best if tackled by two or three children together.

In the case of Activities 3, 4, 5, 6, 7 and 8 discussion will be needed beforehand to point out the use of reference sources to the children, and afterwards to draw their attention to the way they were able to use these sources.

SKILLS TO BE DEVELOPED

Activity 1
The children are here asked to pose questions about their topic from a special point of view. They will probably need some discussion beforehand about the job of a newspaper reporter, and some discussion about the content and style of newspaper reports.

Activity 2
The idea that not all questions are capable of being answered may be unfamiliar to children, and this activity will require a good deal of discussion. It leads well into later work on evaluating evidence.

Activity 3
This is a straightforward information-finding task. It focuses particularly upon the use of an index to locate information.

Activity 4
This activity aims to develop the skills of finding information in reference books. Most of the answers can be obtained by looking up single words in an index or an encyclopaedia. The activity is self-monitoring.

Activity 5
The children are introduced here to a particular way of organising information using a grid format. They also, of course, have to be able to find the information they require. Children often find the grid format difficult and completed grids can be used as a focus for discussion with other children.

Activity 6
This focuses upon the selection of particular items of information which might be buried quite densely in continuous text. As such it is a rather more difficult task than the location of dates or figures. When they have found the information the children are asked to reorganise it into a log-book format.

Activity 7
This introduces the idea of collections of information. It gives an opportunity for practice of location skills as children try to answer the questions. A useful extension would be to introduce the children to data-handling programs on the computer. Their information collections will give a framework for the construction of a computer database.

Activity 8
This activity again requires the location of particular information. The children will be looking for dates and this provides a good opportunity to introduce them to the technique of scanning – that is, glancing quickly at a page to find a specific piece of information. The drawing up of a time-line might be difficult for some of them and may require some preliminary work.

Activity 9
This activity asks children to evaluate evidence they find referred to in books. The concept of evidence may require some discussion. Children may also need some guidance in presenting their evidence in the form of an argument. This might best be done first as an oral activity before moving to writing.

Skills analysis

Topic: Space	Skill stage				
	1	2	3	4	5
Activity 1	√				
Activity 2	√				
Activity 3		√			
Activity 4		√			
Activity 5		√	√	√	
Activity 6		√	√	√	
Activity 7		√	√	√	
Activity 8		√	√	√	
Activity 9		√	√		√

A new star

You are a newspaper reporter looking for a scoop for your newspaper. You have heard that Professor Boffin, the world famous astronomer, has just discovered a new star in the Orion constellation. You want to interview him about it.

Professor Boffin, can I ask you some questions about your discovery?
How big is the new star?
How far away from the earth is it?

What other questions would you want to ask Professor Boffin about the new star? Make a list of the questions you would ask.

After the interview you would use the information you have got from Professor Boffin to write your newspaper report. Can you write the story you think you would produce? Remember to give it an exciting headline so that everyone will want to read it.

© David Wray 1991, *The Project Research Pack*, Stanley Thornes (Publishers) Ltd

Activity 2

Possible and impossible questions

We usually think of questions as being things we can answer. But some questions are impossible to answer.

Read the questions in the list below.

1 How far from the earth is the moon?

2 How many stars are there?

3 How big is the sun?

4 When will we send someone to Mars?

5 Which is the brightest star in the sky?

Which of these questions do you think it is possible to answer? Which are impossible?

You may have realised that it is impossible to know how many stars there are. Space is so big that most people think it could never all be measured and counted.

It is also impossible to know when we will reach Mars. Lots of things may happen to stop us. We cannot predict the future for certain.

Make two headings in your book.

Questions we can answer	Impossible questions

Write some questions about space under each of these headings.

© David Wray 1991, *The Project Research Pack*, Stanley Thornes (Publishers) Ltd

Constellations

A constellation is a group of stars. Many of these groups have been given the names of legendary creatures and people because of their shapes.

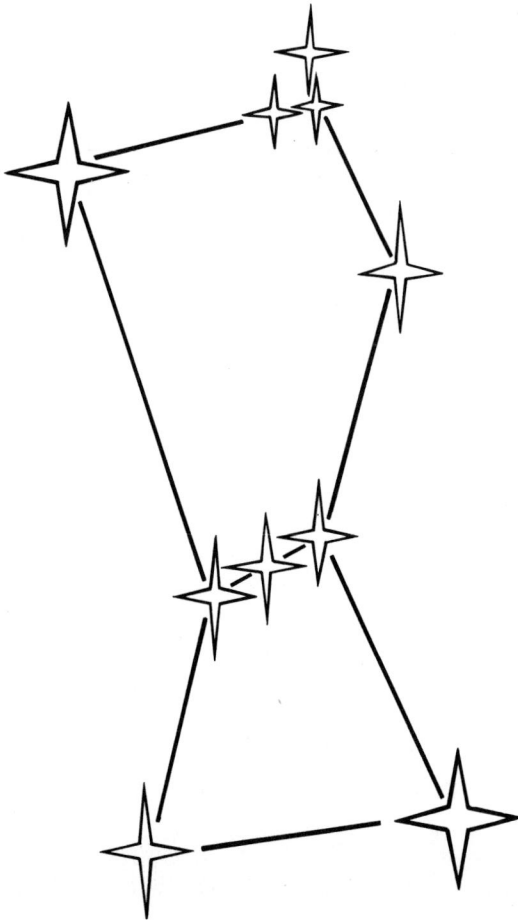

Here is a picture of a famous constellation which we often see in the sky.

Can you find out what the name of this constellation is?

You might also be able to find out the legend of this person.

Here are some more names of constellations. Write each name in your book, and next to it draw a picture of the star shape which makes the constellation. Remember to use the index in each reference book you use.

The Great Bear

Casseopia

The Archer

The Crab

The Bull

© David Wray 1991, *The Project Research Pack*, Stanley Thornes (Publishers) Ltd

Space puzzle

Activity 4

The real name of a shooting star is hidden in the pattern below. To discover it, read each of the sentences carefully. If a sentence is true, colour in the spaces you are told to. If the sentence is not true, do not colour in anything.

1 If the name of the largest planet is Jupiter, colour in the spaces marked **4**.

2 If the nearest planet to the Earth is Saturn, colour in the spaces marked **8**.

3 If people who study space are called astrologers, colour in the spaces marked **0**.

4 If the first man in space was called Yuri Gagarin, colour in the spaces marked **1**.

5 If Venus is known as the red planet, colour in the spaces marked **3**.

6 If the nearest planet to the sun is called Uranus, colour in the spaces marked **9**.

7 If the first man on the moon was called Neil Armstrong, colour in the spaces marked **6**.

8 If the moon takes a year to go round the earth, colour in the spaces marked **2**.

9 If Voyager was a manned space ship, colour in the spaces marked **7**.

10 If the Pole star is in the constellation called the Plough, colour in the spaced marked **5**.

1	6	5	4	3	1	6	5	4	0	1	7	3	2	6	0	1	6	6	5	0	6	5	4
4	9	3	8	7	1	7	0	6	2	6	5	7	1	5	9	5	9	8	7	3	2	1	0
6	9	2	8	8	5	8	2	4	3	1	8	4	9	4	8	6	2	0	2	3	7	6	9
5	7	7	9	9	4	9	3	5	7	6	3	2	0	1	7	4	1	6	8	9	8	4	8
1	8	0	3	3	6	0	7	6	8	5	7	8	9	6	3	6	2	0	3	9	8	6	7
6	0	8	7	7	1	7	8	1	9	4	3	2	0	5	2	5	3	7	8	7	0	5	3
4	5	1	6	8	5	4	1	6	0	6	7	8	9	5	0	1	6	5	4	8	9	4	2

© David Wray 1991, *The Project Research Pack*, Stanley Thornes (Publishers) Ltd

Famous space craft

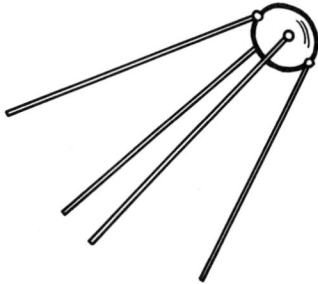

This is a picture of Sputnik, which was the very first space craft to be sent into space. It was unmanned but its launch was very important and marked the beginning of the race into space.

You can begin to collect information about other famous space craft. Here are the names of some to get you started:

> Vostok
> Challenger
> Apollo
> Voyager

Try to add some more to this list.

To build up a dossier on each space craft you will need:

> A picture of the space craft
>
> Information about it, including:
>   the country it came from
>   when it was launched
>   where it went.

When you have found the information you can make a book of space craft. You could try to give your book a contents page and an index.

© David Wray 1991, *The Project Research Pack*, Stanley Thornes (Publishers) Ltd

The space race

Here are some famous events in the history of the race to be the first on the moon. Unfortunately they are in the wrong order. Can you re-arrange them so that the event which happened first is placed first, and so on? Remember to use the index pages of your reference books to help you.

Man first walks in space.

Man walks on the moon.

The first animal is sent into space.

Man first flies in space.

Man orbits the earth.

Two space craft dock in space.

Use these events to begin your own time-line of the race into space. Find some more important events and place them in the right place on your time-line.

These events could be illustrated and would make an interesting booklet for your friends to read.

© David Wray 1991, *The Project Research Pack*, Stanley Thornes (Publishers) Ltd

A planet chart

Down the left hand side of the grid below write the names of the nine planets which orbit our sun.

For each of these planets try to answer the questions along the top of the grid. Put the answers in the correct boxes.

Remember that you will need to use the contents and index pages of the reference books you look in.

Questions / Names of planets	How far from the sun?	How long is its year?	How hot is its surface?	How many moons does it have?
1				
2				
3				
4				
5				
6				
7				
8				
9				

When you have finished it you can use your chart to ask your friends questions such as, 'Which planet is third nearest the sun and has one moon?'

© David Wray 1991, *The Project Research Pack*, Stanley Thornes (Publishers) Ltd

Activity 8

The solar system

The space ship 'Probe II' is being sent on a mission to explore the planets in the solar system. It will travel from Earth to Mars and then onwards to the planets further out.

For each planet it lands on, the captain will send back a log entry containing information about the planet. A log entry will look like this.

Earth date . . . . Year . . . . Planet . . . .

Surface conditions . . . .

. . . .

Temperature . . . .

Other observations . . . .

. . . .

. . . .

Photographs of surface:

Can you write a log book for this journey? Make your entries as true to life as you can. You will find information in your books to help you.

© David Wray 1991, *The Project Research Pack*, Stanley Thornes (Publishers) Ltd

Life on Mars

People have always wondered whether there is life on other planets. Mars is one of the closest planets to us, and it has usually been the favourite place for people to think there is life. There have been many stories about Martians. You may have heard of some of these.

Do you think it is possible that there is life on Mars?

Rather than guess the answer to this question, let us see if we can find any evidence.

Make two headings in your book, like this:

Evidence for life on Mars	Evidence against life on Mars
Astronomers have discovered marks on Mars which look man-made.	There is no oxygen on Mars to support life as we know it.

Look in your books to try to find some evidence for and against there being life on Mars, and make a note of each piece of evidence you find under the right heading. You will see that one piece of evidence has already been placed under each heading.

When you have found several pieces of evidence, decide what you think about the possibility of life on Mars. Then write an account to try to convince someone else that what you think is true.

© David Wray 1991, *The Project Research Pack*, Stanley Thornes (Publishers) Ltd

The weather

USING THE ACTIVITIES

The appropriateness of these activities for particular groups of children will depend upon a number of things, including their previous experience with this kind of work. Teachers are therefore urged to use the activity sheets as they think appropriate. A tentative grading might, however, be as follows:

Lower juniors (ages 7–9): Activities 1, 3, 4, 6
Upper juniors (ages 9–11): Activities 2, 5, 7, 8, 9

These activities can be done as self-contained exercises, but they will all benefit greatly from discussion beforehand, and (especially) afterwards. All the activities will work best if tackled by two or three children together.

In the case of Activities 3, 4, 5 and 6 discussion will be needed beforehand to point out the use of reference sources to the children, and afterwards to draw their attention to the way they were able to use these sources. For sheets 7 and 9 the sources required will be wider than the normal reference books and will include newspapers, magazines and television programmes.

SKILLS TO BE DEVELOPED

Activity 1
The children are here asked to pose questions about their topic from a special point of view. They will probably need some discussion beforehand about the job of a meteorologist, and an ideal beginning to this activity, and to the project in general, would be a visit from a local expert. Children could also be asked to make a special study of TV weather reports over a few days.

Activity 2
This activity focuses upon the planning of the project coverage and the asking of questions. Children should be expected to formulate a list of questions around which they plan a talk. These questions are also guides for their subsequent information finding work.

Activity 3
This activity aims to develop the skills of finding information in reference books. Most of the answers can be obtained by looking up single words in an index or an encyclopaedia, although part of the skill will be in knowing which words to look up. The children should be encouraged to try several alternatives.

Activity 4
Another information-location task which will require the use of indexes and/or dictionaries. Children are asked at the end to design their own crosswords, an activity which has a great deal of potential.

Answers
Across: 1 Degrees. 5 Alaska. 7 p.m. 8 Seven.
  10 Cumulus.
Down: 2 Gale. 3 Easterly. 4 Scale. 6 Space. 9 a.m.

Activity 5
This extends the skills aimed at in the previous activity. The children have to find specific pieces of information about the weather. This information is likely to be buried in some dense text, so children will have to use skimming and scanning techniques. They are introduced to a list-type presentation of information.

Activity 6
A similar kind of activity in which children have to locate selected pieces of information. The activity combines the use of the index with skimming and scanning to locate information.

Activity 7
Here the children are directed to newspapers to find specific information, which they are then encouraged to present in a format which they decide is appropriate. They may need some help with tabular and graphical representations of information.

Activity 8
Here children are asked to find several pieces of information and then to reorganise them into the form of a newspaper report. Many of them will need to be given some experience of reading newspaper reports and discussing their content and style. This could profitably be done as a series of whole class lessons. In writing their reports children might be able to use a newspaper emulation computer programme such as *Front Page Extra*.

Activity 9
Here the children are asked to keep a series of records and compare them with forecasts. This will give them a basis for evaluating the information they come across in weather forecasts, and a greater understanding of the difficulties of accurate prediction.

117

Skills analysis

Topic: The Weather	Skill stage				
	1	2	3	4	5
Activity 1	√				
Activity 2	√				
Activity 3		√			
Activity 4		√			
Activity 5		√	√		
Activity 6		√	√		
Activity 7				√	
Activity 8		√	√	√	
Activity 9				√	√

118

Be a meteorologist

A meteorologist is a person who studies the weather. The meteorologist's job includes:

Keeping records of the weather in different parts of the world;

Making charts to show the way weather systems move around the world;

Making forecasts of the kind of weather particular places can expect.

If you were a meteorologist and had to do all of these things, you would have to begin by deciding what weather records you would keep.

You might want to record these things:

Rainfall in a day

Wind speed and direction.

See if you can add to this list of things to record.

When you have made your list of records to keep, you might be able to try to keep these records for a time.

How will you write them all down so that other people can understand them easily?

© David Wray 1991, *The Project Research Pack*, Stanley Thornes (Publishers) Ltd

Planning a talk

During your project on the weather you might be asked to help give a talk on your topic to another class. When you are planning this talk it will help you to think about the kinds of things you can include in it which are likely to interest your audience.

Make a list of some of the things which you expect the class you will talk to will want to know about weather.

Your list might have on it things like:

> Storms and hurricanes
>
> Snow, frost and hail
>
> Weather forecasting
>
> and other things.

Take each of the things on your list and think of a few questions about each one which you think the audience will be interested in.

For storms and hurricanes, for example, you might have questions like:

What causes hurricanes?

Where is the stormiest place in the world?

What was the most powerful storm ever?

If you do this for all the things you will include in your talk it will help you know what to say about each of them.

Of course, you will have to find out the answers to the questions first!

© David Wray 1991, *The Project Research Pack*, Stanley Thornes (Publishers) Ltd

Weather questions

Activity 3

I have been planning a quiz about the weather. I have a list of interesting questions I want to ask in my quiz. Unfortunately I have not been able to find all the answers, and I think that the answers I have found are in the wrong places. Here is a list of the questions and the answers I have got so far.

QUESTIONS

In which direction do the winds blow in an anti-cyclone?

From which direction do weather systems usually come in Britain?

How cold does the ground have to be before you get a ground frost?

Why is it colder at night than in the daytime?

Why are the tops of mountains colder than the valleys?

What is the record for the hottest place in Britain?

ANSWERS

0 degrees Celsius (0°C)

Because the earth holds heat better than the air

Anti-clockwise

Can you help me sort these out and make a proper weather quiz?

You will need to use some reference books to help you.

You might be able to add some questions to the quiz and test them on your friends.

Activity 4

Weather crossword

Can you complete the crossword below by answering the questions? All the answers have something to do with weather. You will find reference books useful for this. Remember to use the index.

CLUES

Across

1 Temperature is measured in these.
5 The American state with the coldest weather.
7 In the winter in this country it usually gets dark before 5.00 ___.
8 A high wind which is not quite strong enough to be called a gale will be at force ___.
10 The fluffy clouds which form on warm days.

Down

2 At force eight the wind is called a ___.
3 This kind of wind in winter usually means very cold weather in this country.
4 Wind force is measured on the Beaufort ___.
6 Many weather measurements are made from satellites which are in ___.
9 Times in the morning.

Perhaps you can design your own crossword puzzle using words which have something to do with weather. See if your friends can solve it.

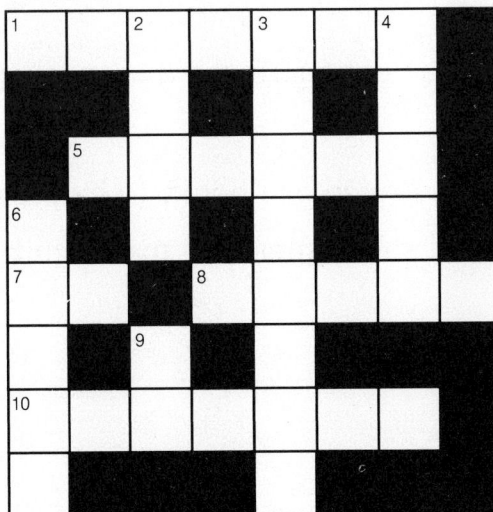

© David Wray 1991, *The Project Research Pack*, Stanley Thornes (Publishers) Ltd

Weather extremes

What is the worst weather you have ever seen?
What is the best weather you have known?

You could find out about some of the worst and best weather the world has had.

Make these headings in your book.

Coldest	Wettest	Hottest	Windiest	Driest

Use your reference books to try to find the coldest place in the world and write its name under the 'Coldest' heading. Can you write down any more information about it, for example, how cold it gets, do people live there and so on.

Do the same thing for the other headings.

These are the weather extremes of the world. What about the weather extremes in our country? Can you find the coldest place in Britain? What about the wettest, hottest and so on?

© David Wray 1991, *The Project Research Pack*, Stanley Thornes (Publishers) Ltd

Clouds

There are many different kinds of clouds. Different kinds of clouds usually mean different kinds of weather.

Here are some names of types of clouds:

cirrus

cirrocumulus

altocumulus

altostratus

cumulus

cumulonimbus

stratus

Can you find pictures of each of these types of clouds?

For each type of cloud find out:

At what height is it usually found?

Why is it given that name?

What kind of weather does it usually mean?

You could use this information to make a booklet on clouds.

© David Wray 1991, *The Project Research Pack*, Stanley Thornes (Publishers) Ltd

Weather records

Most newspapers have a section on weather. In this they usually give:

Weather records for major towns in Britain.

A forecast of the weather for the next day.

Maps of the weather systems over the country.

Using the weather section in any daily newspaper, keep a weather record for a week or two for the large town nearest to you.

You will have to decide on how you will keep your records. You should try to use tables and different kinds of graphs. Discuss with your friends which kind of recording system is best.

Legend

▬▬●▬▬	Warm front	
▬▬▲▬▬	Cold front	
—992—	Isobar with value (hPa)	(ex-millibar)
◑	Indication of cloudiness	(50% in example)
◖	Wind direction & speed	(SW 15 kts)
◉	Calm	
20 ○	Air temperature – deg C	(20 deg C)
●	Sea temperature – deg C	(02 deg C)
⑫●	Weather	(rain)
◖●	Weather	(recent rain)

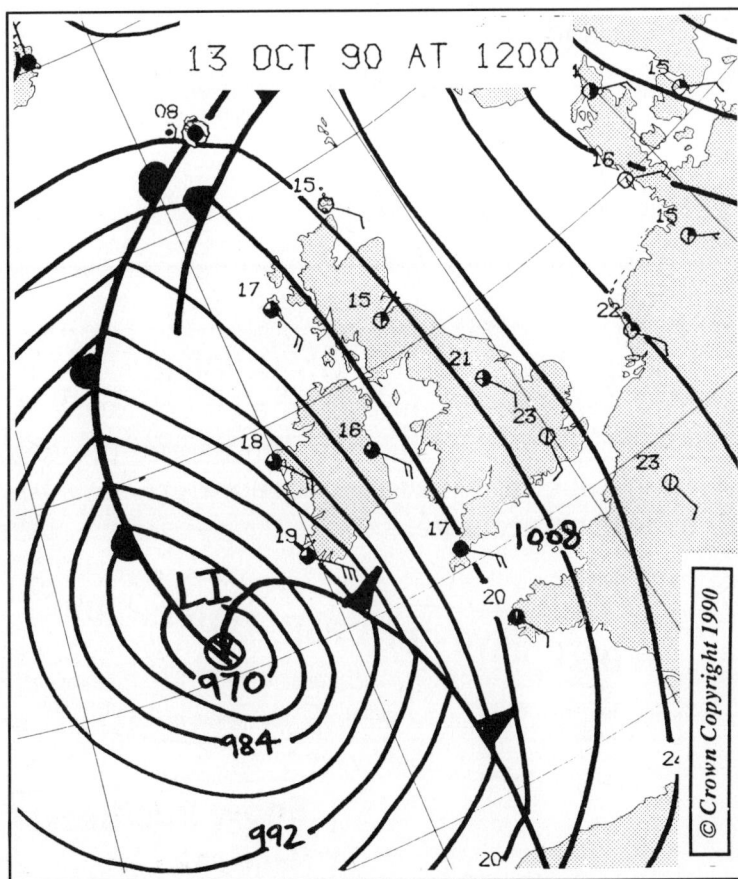

13 OCT 90 AT 1200

© Crown Copyright 1990

© David Wray 1991, *The Project Research Pack*, Stanley Thornes (Publishers) Ltd

Activity 8

Weather disasters

Many disasters are caused by the weather.

Hurricanes do lots of damage.

Heavy rain can cause flooding.

Snow can cause chaos on roads and cut places off completely.

Drought can bring famine.

Choose a weather disaster which has happened recently. You might be able to read about it in newspapers or magazines.

Try to find out:

Where it happened

What caused it

What damage it did

What was done to try to help the people who were affected.

Use the information you have found to write a report on the disaster. You could write your report as if you were a newspaper reporter. Your report will need a headline and some photographs or pictures. Remember that newspaper reporters have to make their reports exciting as well as accurate.

Where have our crisp winters gone?

Weeds are growing wild in England without frosts to mow down verges. Gardeners fear mutant strains and doctors worry about increased incidences of hay-fever with the high pollen count.

Snow Business!

Surprise snow shocks farmers with unexpected losses of lambs. "It's been a worrying winter" Mr MacDonald told *Weather Watch*.

Tropical Temperatures

The Brits are sweltering in record temperatures. Pale with the heat, they are taking off their jackets in droves. "If this blistering weather continues" said Mr Partridge MP "we will need to consider implementing a national siesta."

© David Wray 1991, *The Project Research Pack*, Stanley Thornes (Publishers) Ltd

Activity 9

Weather forecasts

Weather forecasts are given on the television and in newspapers. Many people never believe these forecasts, but how accurate are they? You can find out.

Keep a record of the weather forecasts made on one television channel and in one newspaper for a period of at least ten days.

Keep a record of what the weather was actually like on each of these days.

You will need to record things like:

Temperature

Wind direction

Wind force (light, fairly strong, or very strong)

Did it rain? How long for?

Was it sunny? How long for?

Anything else important?

When you have all this information, try to answer these questions.

Were the weather forecasts accurate?

Was the television forecast more or less accurate than the newspaper?

Can you explain why the weather forecasters do not get their forecasts correct?

You might try making your own forecasts to see how accurate you can be.

Communications

USING THE ACTIVITIES

The appropriateness of these activities for particular groups of children will depend upon a number of things, including their previous experience with this kind of work. Teachers are therefore urged to use the activity sheets as they think appropriate. A tentative grading might, however, be as follows:

Lower juniors (ages 7–9): sheets 1, 3, 5, 7
Upper juniors (ages 9–11): sheets 2, 4, 6, 8, 9

These activities can be done as self-contained exercises, but they will all benefit greatly from discussion beforehand, and (especially) afterwards. All the sheets will work best if tackled by two or three children together.

In the case of Activities 3, 7 and 9 discussion will be needed beforehand to point out the use of reference books to the children, and afterwards to draw their attention to the way they were able to use these books. For Activity 5 they may need some guidance in how to use a language dictionary.

SKILLS TO BE DEVELOPED

Activity 1
This activity is intended to start children thinking about the subject of the project. It will involve them in looking in reference books, not for specific information, but to get a general feel of the subject. This initial browsing can be a useful way of attuning children to the work they will be doing in the project.

Activity 2
This activity focuses upon the planning of the project coverage and the asking of questions. Children should be expected to formulate a list of questions around which they plan a talk. These questions are also guides for their subsequent information finding work.

Activity 3
This activity aims to develop the skills of finding information in reference books. Most of the answers can be obtained by looking up single words in an index or an encyclopaedia, although part of the skill will be in knowing which words to look up. The children should be encouraged to try several alternatives.

Activity 4
This extends the skills developed in the previous activity. The children have to find a copy of the Morse Code in reference books, and then to use this information to solve the problem. The activity could act as the introduction to a great deal of further work on codes and ciphers.

Activity 5
Here the children have to find particular information but in rather different sources. They will require access to language dictionaries, although they may be able to get these from home. The activity could be usefully extended into a more general look at languages, especially if there are children in the class who speak languages other than English.

Activity 6
The children are asked here to use and reorganise the information they find in an everyday source. The activity is reasonably simple although it asks them to see things from others' points of view, which may be new to them.

Activity 7
This activity again requires information to be selected and then organised in particular ways. Some of the information the children need will be found from personal experience or from asking other people. These are important sources of information which should not be neglected.

Activity 8
This activity introduces children to the evaluation of information by asking them to produce 'persuasive' information deliberately. Doing this should raise their awareness of how information can be presented in this way, and, hopefully, make them more circumspect about it in the real world. Advertisement designing has many applications in primary schooling.

Activity 9
Here the children are asked to evaluate information and opinions they find in their books. They might usefully be given magazine material for this activity, since this tends to be more up to date and polemical than most reference books.

Skills analysis

Topic: Communications	Skill stage				
	1	2	3	4	5
Activity 1	√				
Activity 2	√				
Activity 3		√			
Activity 4		√	√		
Activity 5		√	√		
Activity 6		√	√	√	
Activity 7			√	√	
Activity 8					√
Activity 9			√		√

129

Many media

We communicate with other people in many different ways.

We can:

Talk to them

Use mime

Use a telephone

and many other ways. These ways are called 'media'.

Can you make this list longer?

Add to it all the ways you can find which we use to communicate.

Show your list to a friend. Your friend might be able to give you some more suggestions to add to your list.

Do you know how each of these media works? There will probably be lots of questions you would like to ask about all these media. Start making a list of these questions now.

© David Wray 1991, *The Project Research Pack*, Stanley Thornes (Publishers) Ltd

Planning a talk

During your project on communications you might be asked to help give a talk on your topic to another class. When you are planning this talk it will help you to think about the kinds of things you can include in it which are likely to interest your audience.

Make a list of some of the things which you expect the class you will talk to will want to know about communications.

Your list might have on it things like:

> Television
> Video
> Codes
> Satellites
>
> and other things.

Take each of the things on your list and think of a few questions for each one that you think the audience will be interested in. For television, for example, you might have questions like:

How does a television work?
Who invented television?
When was the first television programme made?

If you do this for all the things you will include in your talk it will help you know what to say about each of them.

Of course, you will have to find out the answers to the questions first!

© David Wray 1991, *The Project Research Pack*, Stanley Thornes (Publishers) Ltd

A broken computer

I have been using my computer to help me answer some difficult questions about communications. I think, though, that it must be broken, because it has not given me all the answers and the answers it has given me seem a bit mixed up. Here are the questions I asked and the answers the computer gave.

QUESTIONS	ANSWERS
Who invented television?	Semaphore
What does BBC stand for?	A transmitter
Which signalling system uses flags?	Dutch
What language is spoken in Holland?	
What do we call the writing system of the Ancient Egyptians?	
If a receiver receives messages, what machine sends them?	

Can you help me sort these out and get right answers to all my questions? You will need to use some reference books to help you.

© David Wray 1991, *The Project Research Pack*, Stanley Thornes (Publishers) Ltd

Activity 4

Morse code

Sam Smart, the spy, was very pleased with himself the other day when he intercepted a message from his enemy. He thinks the message is in Morse Code, but the enemy has not left any gaps between the letters. Can you help Sam work out the code? You will need to find a book with the Morse Code in.

———.....—.—.————.—...—.....—.—..—.....—.—.

—....—.......—..—.—.....——..—..——...————...——.....—

If Sam can decipher the message he will send a false message back to his enemy in the same code, saying 'Message received. Contact Sam Smart, our new friend.' Can you put this in code for him?

Sam also wanted to send a message in another code to his assistant to say, 'I have set a trap for the enemy.' He sent the following message.

JIBWFTFUBUSBQGPSUIFFOFNZ

Can you work out what sort of code Sam has used?

Try sending messages to your friends using this code or any other code you can find. See if your friends can decipher your new code.

© David Wray 1991, *The Project Research Pack*, Stanley Thornes (Publishers) Ltd

Hello, hello!

If you wanted to say 'Hello' to someone in France, you would say:

Bon jour.

In Spain you would say:

Buenos días

Can you find out how you would say 'Hello' in:

Italian

German

Russian

Welsh

and any other language you can? You might find out by looking in reference books about these countries, or by using special language dictionaries.

Think of some other useful words which you could find out how to say in these languages. Perhaps you could start with 'Goodbye'. See how much of the chart below you can fill in. Use the blank slots for other languages and words you want to add.

Word \ Language	Italian	German	Russian	Welsh	
Hello					
Goodbye					
School					

© David Wray 1991, *The Project Research Pack*, Stanley Thornes (Publishers) Ltd

Planning for the television

Imagine you were going to spend an evening watching television with the following people:

Aunt Jane, who likes programmes about animals and news programmes, but hates pop music programmes and sport,

Uncle John, who likes soap operas and films, but hates news and music programmes,

Cousin Jim, who likes everything apart from pop music programmes which drive him wild,

Cousin Julie, who only likes soap operas, but who would rather read than watch television anyway,

and you know what *you* like and hate on television.

Using a copy of the television programme guide for tonight, try to plan an evening's viewing which will please as many of these people as possible (including yourself).

After doing this, you might like to think of some other people you know and see if you could plan an evening's viewing for them.

© David Wray 1991, *The Project Research Pack*, Stanley Thornes (Publishers) Ltd

Animal communication

Human beings are not the only creatures to communicate with each other. Animals also communicate, but they do it in different ways. Humans communicate mainly through speaking to each other, but animals cannot speak so they use other senses.

Some animals communicate through sound.   Dogs bark to show they are angry.

Some animals communicate through sight.   Peacocks spread their tails to impress their mates.

Some animals communicate through smell.   Cats leave scents to mark out their territories.

Some animals communicate through touch.   Cats rub against us to show they are pleased.

Make four headings in your book, like this:

Sound	Sight	Smell	Touch

Under each heading write down a few examples of how animals communicate through this. You will need to use your reference books and encyclopaedias to help you. You might also get some information by asking people, especially people who keep animals.

© David Wray 1991, *The Project Research Pack*, Stanley Thornes (Publishers) Ltd

Design an advert

Think of a new product you would like to invent. It might be a new toy, a new kind of sweet, a new game or anything you like.

When you have decided on your product, think about how you would advertise this if you wanted other people to buy it.

To help you do this it would be useful to collect some examples of advertisements for products like yours which you might find in magazines, newspapers or on television. How do these advertisements go about trying to persuade people to buy products?

When you have looked at lots of advertisements for other products, try to design some advertisements for your own. These might be the kind of advertisements you would see in magazines, or you might be able to make a short video advertisement, or a radio advertisement using a tape-recorder.

After making your advertisements you need to try them out on your friends. Ask your friends if the advertisements made them want to buy your product, and why. This might give you some clues about how you might redesign your advertisement.

COME CLEAN WITH SUDSO!

– the kindest washing powder.

*It cares
for your whole family wash,*

cleaning
WHITER
BRIGHTER
SOFTER.

The gentle power of SUDSO will lift dirt from even the grimiest collars and cuffs.

100% natural. SUDSO – the greenest, cleanest washing powder.

© David Wray 1991, *The Project Research Pack*, Stanley Thornes (Publishers) Ltd

Communication 2000

Many of the ways in which we communicate today have only begun to be used in the past 100 years. 100 years ago nobody had heard of television, radio, telephones or computers. It may be that in the next 100 years we will find other ways of communicating which none of us know about yet.

Many of the reference books you have been using for your project on communications will have suggestions for how communications might change in years to come. Collect some of these predictions and sort them into two lists, using the headings below. I have started each list off, although you might not agree with me about these things.

Predictions I think will come true	Predictions I do not think will come true
Instead of telephones we will use videophones.	Because everyone will have computers, we will not need any books.

© David Wray 1991, *The Project Research Pack*, Stanley Thornes (Publishers) Ltd

Presentation activities

Presentation activities

The six sheets included in this section suggest ways in which children might present their project work to other audiences. Sometimes there may be special reasons why one form of presentation is more appropriate than others, and at other times the children can be allowed simply to choose the form of presentation they prefer.

The six forms of presentation covered in these sheets are:

1 Preparing a talk
2 Writing a book
3 Designing a wall-chart
4 Making a cassette
5 A slide presentation
6 Mounting a display

The sheets are intended as resource material and are not expected to be followed slavishly. Perhaps the most valuable way of using them is to allow children to adapt the ideas and then produce their own presentation guidelines for other children to use.

Preparing a talk

You might present the work you have done on your project by giving a talk about it to some other people. This talk will need to be carefully planned. You will need to:

1 Think about who is going to listen to the talk.

If the talk is for children younger than you are you will need to make it simple enough for them to understand.

If the people listening to the talk have been doing the same project as you, you will not need to tell them about things they already know.

2 Think about what you will include in your talk.

You will not have time to include everything you have done in your project. You will have to choose.

Try to choose the most interesting parts to talk about, but make sure your talk makes good sense and does not jump around from thing to thing.

3 Think about how you will present your talk.

Presenting information just by talking can be a bit dull. Can you include pictures, models or extracts from tape-recordings? If you can this will make it more interesting.

4 Write yourself a script.

You will need to have something to remind you of what comes next in your talk. It is best, though, if you do not just read your script out loud. Try to remember as much of it as you can.

Good Luck!

© David Wray 1991, *The Project Research Pack*, Stanley Thornes (Publishers) Ltd

Writing a book

One way of presenting all the information you have found during your project is to make it into a book. This needs a lot of thinking about. The following questions will help you make a start.

1 Who is the book going to be for?

It might be for your friends to read, or to take home to your parents, or to give to the children in the infants so that they can read it. Whichever it is you will need to make sure that they can read it.

2 What is going to be in the book?

You need to plan out the chapters the book will have and begin by writing a contents page for the book.

3 What will be in each chapter?

Each chapter needs planning before you write it. You will probably need to split it up into several sections.

4 How will you write the book?

Will you use pen and paper, or will you be able to use the word-processor? Will you write a draft of each chapter first before doing it again in your best handwriting? How many pictures or diagrams will you need and how will you do these?

5 What will the book look like?

You might try giving it a hard cardboard cover and binding it with thread and glue. Perhaps your teacher will show you how to do this. The cover will need decorating. Remember that books always have the names of their authors at the beginning.

6 How will you persuade other people to read your book?

You might design an advertisement for your book. This should make it seem really interesting and exciting so that people will want to read it.

© David Wray 1991, *The Project Research Pack*, Stanley Thornes (Publishers) Ltd

Designing a wall-chart

One way of presenting the information you have found out in your project is by making a wall-chart. Here is one way of doing this. Imagine you have been finding out about jobs on the railways.

Make a list of the jobs people do on the railways. Your list might begin with train driver, porter, station announcer . . .

Get a blank piece of card or paper to use for your wall-chart. Roughly divide it into sections, one for each of the jobs you have listed. Your chart might look something like this:

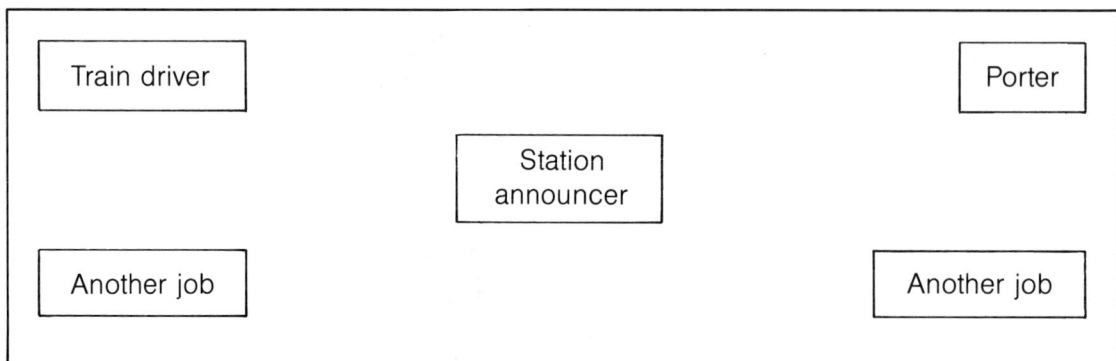

Train driver		Porter
	Station announcer	
Another job		Another job

For each section you need to plan what to include on the chart. You will probably need a picture or photograph of a person doing the job, and you will also need a description of what the job involves. You do not need to include *all* the information you have about each job. You can always use the information you do not have room for on the wall-chart in some other way, perhaps in a booklet.

Remember that a wall-chart has to attract people's attention, so you need to think about how to make it do this. Think about big headings, bright colours and interesting information.

This idea can be altered to suit other information. You could do a wall-chart on:

Famous aeroplanes
Animals in the zoo
The lives of the Vikings

and lots of other things.

© David Wray 1991, *The Project Research Pack*, Stanley Thornes (Publishers) Ltd

Making a cassette

To present some of your project work you might be able to make a cassette. You could do this so that it sounds like a radio programme. You will need to think of several things.

1 What to include?

Do not try to include too much material. The best cassette programmes last no longer than 30 minutes. It is best to leave your listeners interested and wanting more.

2 What sections to have?

You will probably need several sections of about five minutes each. Do not spend too long on one section so your audience does not get bored with it.

Try also to vary the kinds of sections you have. It is best to mix up serious and funny sections. If you cannot think of a funny section perhaps you could include a joke in between each of the serious sections. This will help keep the audience alert.

3 Planning.

You need to plan carefully what you will have in your programme. Write down a list of items with times against them, remembering to plan for variety.

4 Rehearse.

Rehearse each section well before you begin to record it. When you are recording it is best if the people taking part know their parts off by heart rather than reading them from a sheet.

5 Try things out.

If you have a chance, try out the sections you have recorded on other people. They might give you some ideas for improving things.

It can be great fun making a cassette. Remember that you are doing it so that other people can also have fun listening to it.

© David Wray 1991, *The Project Research Pack*, Stanley Thornes (Publishers) Ltd

A slide presentation

An interesting way of presenting your project work is by showing a series of slides. There are two ways of doing this.

1 Photographs.

You can take photographs and have them developed as slides. These can include photographs of places you have visited as part of your project, or of the work you have produced.

2 Overheads.

You can make overhead projector slides if you have an overhead projector in your school. You can draw and write on these slides.

When you have made your slides and decided which ones you want to show, you will need to prepare a commentary to go with them. This can be presented in two ways.

A It can be read out as the slides are shown.

B You can record it on tape so that you can play it back as the slides are shown. If you do this remember to include signals on the tape to tell you when to change slide.

Do not try to include too many slides in your presentation. It is best if the presentation lasts no longer than half an hour. Test it before you present it for real to see if it is too long.

© David Wray 1991, *The Project Research Pack*, Stanley Thornes (Publishers) Ltd

Activity 6 — Mounting a display

One way of presenting the work you do in your project is to mount a display for everyone to look at. When you plan a display there are several things you need to think about.

1 What space have you got?

You may just have a section of the classroom wall. This will mean your display can include only paintings, posters and writing.

Can you get a table to put in front of your display? If you can you will be able to include in your display models, books and things for people to touch. These will make your display much more interesting.

2 What material have you got?

You will probably have some written work and some paintings or drawings. If you can include some of these things your display will look more interesting:

Models
Books
Diagrams
Quiz questions
Interesting objects.

3 How can you make the display attractive?

Think about other displays which you have seen which were attractive. Can you copy any of their ideas? You might be able to:

give your display an interesting background, such as coloured drapes, set it out so that everything can be seen and it does not look cluttered, include questions and captions to try to make other people do something with your display.

You have worked very hard on your project. It is worth spending some time on your display so that everyone can see how hard you have worked.

© David Wray 1991, *The Project Research Pack*, Stanley Thornes (Publishers) Ltd